ANUNNAKI HISTORY
THE MAGIC OF BABYLON
NEW STANDARD ZUIST EDITION

POCKET EDITION

Published from
Mardukite Borsippa HQ, San Luis Valley, Colorado
Founding Church of Mardukite Zuism,
Mardukite Academy & Systemology Society
for religious and educational purposes only.

ANUNNAKI HISTORY

THE MAGIC OF BABYLON

NEW STANDARD ZUIST EDITION

Developed by Joshua Free for the
Church of Mardukite Zuism

THE JOSHUA FREE IMPRINT
JFI PUBLICATIONS

ISBN : 978-1-961-50901-6

A special pocket version of
Ancient Babylonian Magic (Liber-51)
edited for founding the
Church of Mardukite Zuism

Pocket Paperback Edition — *June 2023*

Also available in hardcover as
"Babylonian Myth & Magic"

mardukite.com

The _Original_ History and Magic of Planet Earth

Long-lost secrets of ancient Mesopotamian magic and Babylonian mythology drawn from cuneiform tablets are revealed to all in this special pocket paperback edition of the original Mardukite guide to esoteric Anunnaki Spirituality of Babylon and Sumer.

Even if you think you already know all about the Babylonian StarGates and Sumerian History...

Here you will find a beautifully crafted tradition unlike any other legacy Humans have had an opportunity to experience for thousands of years.

Here you'll find an insightful tome demonstrating a refreshing approach, using ancient spirituality for practicing modern Mesopotamian Neopaganism.

Here is a Master Key to the ancient mystic arts; continuing further on that spiritual journey, which began with 'Anunnaki Gods: Sumerian Religion', as inspired by 'Anunnaki Bible' research —true knowledge concerning celestial powers and the Star-Gates dedicated to Anunnaki entities.

Here is the New Standard Zuist Edition of the classic text by world renowned Joshua Free; a pocket paperback version of the original "Babylonian Myth and Magic" (Liber-51) edited for the Church of Mardukite Zuism.

TABLET OF CONTENTS

10TH ANNIVERSARY INTRODUCTION

by Joshua Free

The Mardukite Chamberlains (Mardukite Research Organization) completed its Year-1 cycle of work in early 2010—and those efforts culminated into an anthology first released as *"Necronomicon: The Anunnaki Bible"*—but which, for a recent solidification of our tradition as Mardukite Zuism, has also been published as *"The Complete Anunnaki Bible"*; and even a newly revised pocket-portable abridged format, *"Anunnaki Bible: The Cuneiform Scriptures (New Standard Zuist Edition),"* is available. That culmination of material has certainly earned its recognition as a critical staple and source book for a modern Mardukite revival, even now, over a decade later.

Although a necessary foundation to work from, completion of the Year-1 (2009) work proved to be only a beginning for the route that would carry and build a global underground spiritual movement, now, into the 2020's and beyond with a revitalized "religious brand" as *Mardukite Zuism* and its very effective *Systemology* of applied spiritual technology. Much of this would not have been possible—or even coherently relevant—were it not for the pivotal Year-2 (2010) continuation of efforts made by "Chamberlains Alumni," those that dedicated another year of attention to the practical esoteric interpretation of the *"Anunnaki Bible"* and its background.

In 2010, the "Mardukite Chamberlains" began publishing an esoteric history series by Joshua Free, establishing stronger foundations for the modern revival interest. This included "Liber-50" (released as *"Sumerian Religion"* and *"The Gates of the Necronomicon"*), "Liber-W" (*"The Book of Marduk by Nabu"*) and "Liber-M" (*"Maqlu Ritual Book"*)—all of which have been reissued as 10th Anniversary Collector's Hardcovers.

However, the actual series conclusion appeared in 2011, with "Liber-51" and "Liber-E"—which were combined and reissued in hardcover as *"Babyloni-an Myth & Magic."* And the first portion of this —"Liber-51"—finally appears in this *New Standard Zuist Edition* that you now hold. The second portion will be released in pocket paperback as *"Anunnaki Origins: The Epic of Creation."*

10TH ANNIVERSARY FOREWORD

"The Gates-Games of Marduk"
by David Zibert

The esoteric concept of *"Gates"*—*Gateways* or *Star-Gates*—is a central theme in Babylonian lore and its later derivatives. Oftentimes, these are symbolically interpreted by "mystics" and "magicians" as *Thresholds* connecting between alternate (or parallel) "dimensions," "planes" or "realities."

During most occult initiation processes, the *Seeker* is guided through a series of specific dramatic ceremonial enactments in the Physical Universe that are intended to correlate with a Spiritual Universe, as per the famous Hermetic doctrine of "AS ABOVE, SO BELOW,"[1] leading an initiate through a kind of labyrinthine spiritual/mind maze —a "game" whereby the magician or priest seeks Ascension by moving through such symbolic *Gateways* and *Tunnels*.[2] These types of "games" are often referred to as "Magickal Pathworking"

---

1   While famously attributed to Hermes Trismegistus, this quote is originally found on an older Babylonian *cuneiform* tablet; see *"Tablets of Destiny (Revelation)"* (*Liber-One*) by Joshua Free.

2   Different semantics exist for the concept of *Gates* (described here) in every ancient culture across the globe. These may be readily and easily researched, if the *Seeker* is so inclined.

or *Gatewalking*. Such a concept, in one form or another, will undoubtedly be already familiar to those acquainted with the occult underground; yet many times, a modern practitioner is likely to overlook the actual nature and significance of these *Gates*.

Sure enough, the very use of "*Gate*" semantics—*Thresholds*, *Portals* or any kind of *Door*—to represent another dimension or reality, is merely a *symbol* for the mind (or control center) to process data from a higher frequency of *Beingness*—the data coming from the *other side* of the *Gate*—down to the physical (*beta*) reality. A *symbol* is never the "thing" symbolized. The *symbol* is a *symbol*; and that is all there is to it.

> *Symbols* are frequently misunderstood
> *to be* equal to that which they represent.

So, this begs-the-question: Why exactly are practitioners using semantics and symbols of *Gates* in the first place? What is a *Gate*? A kind of *doorway*? Okay, what then about that? Perhaps a "door" is a type of intermediary *opening* between two different places or points in space...maybe? That seems rather legit if looking at and considering a bit of the aforementioned "games" and how they work—and these can get pretty involved; and there's nothing wrong with that. *Except for one point*: that's not actually what a "door" is at all!

And those beings—those who designed the rules of this "game" are taking great care that everyone is too distracted by the systems to notice that. They are, in fact, counting on this to keep the "game" alive. Simply stated:

> A "*door*" is a willfully built and directed *opening* through a willfully built and directed *barrier*.

That's all there is to *that*. Now, apply *that* to the "games" being played out in this universe, and realize how someone, somewhere, has intentionally put those barriers up, making you believe that he's some kind of authority over yourself, the real Self, and that you absolutely have to move through some maze like a mouse to see the Light at the end of the tunnel, when all you have to do is simply take back responsibility for playing the "game" and remove these barriers you were enforced to be in agreement with; to actually meet-up with your true Self and realize that in the holistic nature of spiritual (*Alpha*)[3] existence, that the "Clear Light" was there all along. *Do you see that?*

---

3   Semantics of "Alpha" and "Beta" existence and "control centers" are derived from "*Mardukite Systemology*" materials; "*Mardukite Zuism: A Brief Introduction*" is found in this present book.

* * * * * * *

The way the "game" of physical (*beta*) reality is set up is demonstrated in the Babylonian *Epic of Creation*—the *Enuma Eliš*—where MARDUK endeavored to order the physical (*beta*) universe/reality through what is described as the fashioning and sealing of *Gates*. The famous *Epic* relates how control over the game of reality is somehow bound to the control of some nebulous "*Tablets of Destiny*," which, in the beginning, are in possession of TIAMAT.

The *Enuma Eliš* is not only the Archetypal *Epic of Creation*, it's also the Archetypal "*Fantasy Adventure*" where a hero goes to slay an evil dragon in order to retrieve a magical treasure. TIAMAT is the "evil one" in this instance, but more accurately, she has the *Tablets of Destiny*—and MARDUK succeeded in convincing his fellow *Anunnaki* to agree for him to direct his attention toward being the maker of the rules, the setter of barriers—the "*Game-Master.*" In view of the *Epic*: should MARDUK succeed in slaying the dragon, he is promised to have ultimate authority over creation, bypassing the Cosmic Law of causality by somehow getting the other *Anunnaki*—and then later on, *Humanity*—to willfully agree to said authority; the very way to make up the rules...

"The ANUNNAKI told MARDUK:
Thy fate is unequaled, thy word is ANU.
Your words shall be command,
In your power shall it be to exalt and to
  abase.
None among the gods shall transgress your
  boundary."

—*"Enuma Eliš,"* Tablet-IV

"The ANUNNAKI set out a garment
And continued to speak to MARDUK.
'May thy fate, O lord, be supreme among the
  gods,
To destroy and to create; speak only the
  word,
And your command shall be fulfilled.
Command now that the garment vanish;
Speak the word again and let the garment
  reappear!'
Then he spake the words and the garment
  vanished;
Again he commanded it and the garment
  reappeared."

—*"Enuma Eliš,"* Tablet-IV

Even before engaging KINGU and TIAMAT in
battle, it is seen that the powers of MARDUK
come first from his own *Self-Determinism* to act—
and be at *Cause*—in the political-play of the

"*gods.*" MARDUK is described as the *only* member of the *Anunnaki* willing to take any *Responsibility* in this matter. By doing so, he directs his *Will* "against all odds" in a grand attempt to become the rule-maker of the "game":

> "All the *gods* have turned to [TIAMAT],
>   with those, whom you created,
> They go to her side. I sent ANU,
>   but he could not withstand her;
> NUDIMMUD[4] was afraid and turned back.
> But MARDUK has set out, the champion of
>   the gods, your son;
> To set out against TIAMAT his heart has
>   called him."
>
> —"*Enuma Eliš*," Tablet-III

> "If I [MARDUK], your avenger,
> Conquer TIAMAT and give you life, [...]
> With my word in place, I will decree fate.
> May whatsoever I do remain unaltered,
> May the word of my lips never be changed
>   nor made to no avail."
>
> —"*Enuma Eliš*," Tablet-III

---

4   An alternate name for ENKI, meaning "*The Fashioner.*"

Now I hope this won't be a spoiler for newcomers, but MARDUK does successfully gain control of the *Tablets of Destiny*, simultaneously killing TIAMAT and her brood. MARDUK's overtaking of physical reality is clear as TIAMAT loses touch with the consensual reality that she just previously had dominion over, the tablets stating: "[…] she acted possessed and lost her sense of reason." The remainder of the *Epic* describes how MARDUK set up rules of his own by "*postulating*" a reality based on agreements about "*barriers*," or else, *something to be free from*—pretty carceral[5] stuff alright: the *Gates* system—or *Matrix*—underlying physical (*beta*) reality to this day. But, MARDUK is a clever fellow—and, of course, he just left the *Key* to the *Locks* around for us, in plain sight:

> "With the *Key* known only to my *Race*.
> Let none enter that *Gate*,
> Since to invoke *Death* is to utter the final prayer."

> —"*Enuma Eliš*," Tablet-VI

So while it might seem to some that the efforts of MARDUK relayed within the *Enuma Eliš* is what has entrapped humanity into this existence as some kind of "evil demiurge"—which is the view taken by the original "Gnostics" and their derivati-

---

5 "*Carceral*" – of, or pertaining to, a prison or imprisonment.

ves—it is not so. The Babylonian *Epic of Creation* is rather a gift of MARDUK to humanity. It contains the *Keys* of reality systematization and its engineering; how it is done, but also how it can be undone.

These *Arcane Tablets* composing the *Creation Epic* relate, quite simply, "*Creation*"—that is, something willfully and purposefully "made" by an *Awareness*. We are now able to clearly see the systematic pattern behind such Creation, then undo and redo it under full *Responsibility of Self*.

And that's what "Mardukite Systemology" *is*.

That is what is meant by "using ancient wisdom to unlock human potential."

MARDUK is thus the Archetypal *Alpha Spirit*[6] incarnated. Here is why it is said, in the celebrated Mardukite Incantation of Eridu: "It is not I, but MARDUK who commands the incantation." This method does not mean a surrendering of the Self to an outside force that is personified by a godform. it is taking back contact with the real *Self*—

6   *"Alpha Spirit"* – a spiritual lifeform; the True Self or "I-AM"; the spirit that is controlling the physical body (genetic vehicle) using a Lifeline, or continuum, of spiritual "ZU" energy. Refer to *"Mardukite Zuism: A Brief Introduction."*

the *Alpha Self*—of which MARDUK is a demonstration of.

Actuality of the literal events in the tale itself becomes irrelevant; because a workable method of reaching higher realities has been drawn from it.

And what is workable *is* true.

The *Enuma Eliš* is not only the *Epic of Creation* for a Physical (*Beta*) Universe, but also the *creation of human ability* to reclaim Self. Everyone carries within Self the potential to be MARDUK. This means you and I, here and now, have the right to awaken this potential as it was foretold on these *Arcane Tablets*.

It has always been there.

All you have to do is *remember*.

Spirit of the Earth, remember!
Spirit of the Sky, remember!

~ David Zibert
Master Mardukite of Canada
Council of Nabu-Tutu
Systemology A.T. Lab Office, Québec
Summer Solstice 2021

INTRODUCTION TO THE 2011 EDITION

*"An Introduction to Esoteric Archaeology
in the 21st Century"*

Mystics of every age go forth explaining an almost *quantum* vision of reality and existence: entangled, interconnected—*All-as-One.* In physical existence, facets tend to be correlated and knowledge is based on *"associations."* Our brand of esoteric archaeology is often considered an obscure approach to crossing the threshold of what is otherwise only treated as an "academic" topic, dry and irrelevant for our times; it is not. Consider for a moment that our *mythic past* is very much rooted in *truth*—albeit misunderstood, but a *truth* that has been conveniently, or forcefully, forgotten among mass awareness and lost to public "exoteric" understanding.

Politics and the general *human condition* evolving, or more accurately, continuing to socially develop outside of the *Ancient Mystery School,* have throughout history, taken its toll on accounts of said *truth*, as becomes quite evident when a *Seeker* sifts the sands to examine shadowy histories of the geographic region known as *Mesopotamia.*

Humans, accepting a *mortal* paradigm, are unaware of one critical aspect of the cosmos—one that they can not see with limited perceptions and reality experiences schematized by semantic labeling—that *Universal Truth*, back of what we experience and treat as knowledge, is actually *unchanging*. Some have even put forth to call it "Cosmic Law."

In spite of the best (or worst) human efforts across time, the *Truth* has survived to remind us of our origins, to instruct us on where we have to go and perhaps, most importantly, the standards we should live by to get there. Mere survival of *Secret Doctrines* by select cabals is not enough. For as the world was once plummeted into *Dark Ages* only to be *reincarnated* in an *Age of Enlightenment*, the "esoteric" *truth* did not resurface in public "exoteric" consciousness—in fact, it went the other direction: *underground* and into *vaults* of obscure "occult" factions. Modern efforts of Mardukite Zuism and its Spiritual Systemology has provided greater clarity.

Original and intended meaning behind esoteric symbolism, used to preserve the integrity of *mysteries*, became as confounded and obscured to the mystical practitioners and "magicians" as the nature of their own organizations, which failed to duplicate a perfect understanding from the *Ancient Mystery School* over thousands of years. But, what's more: they *convinced* themselves that they *did* have true comprehension of it—and so, eventually, politics reflecting the surface world became no less existent in the underground. As above; so below ...*apparently*.

Quests to satisfy an innate desire to pursue *truth*, particularly what has been known as the *Secret of the Ages*, are as obvious in realms of science and academia as they are in the world of the occultist. "Esotericists" are not the only ones interested in unearthing these matters, nor are they even the first ones to pursue such quests for *truth*. Only methodologies and intentions differ. And yet again —*all is connected*.

Without intellectual and scholarly pursuits by historians and academicians, we might have far fewer clues to reconstruct our *mental image* of the past. Where then would the *truth seeker* turn to draw inspiration? From fanciful distortions of pantheism and anthropomorphic fairy-tales passed around by the uninitiated? Certainly, not.

Recovery of the *truth* of mankind's past is paramount to understanding humanity's destined future. It should come as no surprise then that the geographical region associated with its origins remains victim to unyielding war and suffering for thousands of years—further enshrouding our efforts to unveil with a patina of public hesitation and doubt painted by political opinions toward modern *Middle East* activity.

For our current esoteric purposes of the Mardukite movement, our focus is restricted to what academicians call the *Ancient Near East*—or more specifically: *Mesopotamia*.

For over a century, modern pursuit of the *Great Babylonian Mysteries* remained primarily restricted to two approaches:

– Firstly, the late 19th century archaeological excavations inspiring academic Exoteric Assyriology; and the

– Second, derived from the same, made crude esoteric attempts at reviving a working understanding.

> In the first, no attempt is made at philosophical or mystical pragmatism; the entire field of study left as dry as the desert sands it is drawn from.
>
> In the second, early works of these stoic academicians are used at face value to base a revival mystical tradition—often giving little regard for *specifics* of the *system* and effectively requiring many additional facets of knowledge directly appearing nowhere on the same fractured clay tablets and artifacts excavated from these ancient sites.

Fortunately, the 21st century *truth seeker* has a *third* option to explore.

In 2008, a revolutionary (or evolutionary) esoteric underground organization known as the "Mardukites" appeared, publicly visible, and a completely new breed of *next generation* "Esoteric Assyriologists" emerged on the scene—one that would not blindly accept the given data from their predecessors—at least not at *face value*.

For over a decade the diversely organized Mardukite Research Organization sought out the most ancient writings rendered on clay tablets from *Babylonia*—those of which are supportive of the Mardukite movement and contributing to a complete Anunnaki legacy, were eventually published as a source book for our esoteric research library.

Perhaps the most famous and widely circulating volume of our Mardukite Esoteric Research Library is an underground classic available as "*The Complete Anunnaki Bible*," but which was first released as "*Necronomicon: The Anunnaki Bible*" in 2009. It has since been expanded and revised; most recently abridged in portable pocket format as "*Anunnaki Bible: The Cuneiform Scriptures (New Standard Zuist Edition)*.

Other supportive materials were later developed from the Mardukite Esoteric Research Library, including "*Sumerian Religion*" (*Liber-50*), "*The*

Book of Marduk by Nabu" (*Liber-W*), "*The Maqlu Ritual Book*" (*Liber-M*), and additional discourses appearing as: "*Babylonian Myth & Magic*" (*Liber-51*) and "*Magan Magic*" (*Liber-E*). A later present-ation of "*Necronomicon Revelations*" (*Liber-R*) began to reshift the upper-level emphasis onto the future development of what is now publicly visible as Mardukite Systemology.

The entire body of writings collected together for our research library spanning many "Grades" of esoteric study (as published from the *Joshua Free Imprint*) demonstrate an integral link directly between the most ancient origins and the remain-ing evolution or development of human civilization. Our chosen method and the resulting clarity revealed concerning the identity, nature and progression of this *incredible* subject matter show undeniable superiority to what was previously available. But, that is what we call *progress* (much needed for this field).

* * * * * * *

The *Mardukite* approach to reconstructing the *Babylonian* vision begins with first revealing the incredible misnomer that the field of study has en-dured far too long, for essentially, the applicable term "Assyriology" is a *lie*. It's not even semantic-ally correct for our current pursuits of *analysis* using the same physical *evidences* brought to light by late 19th and early 20th century archeology.

The name "Assyriology" questionably applies to this field at all! And although some early scholars acknowledge this grave misrepresentation in labeling the science, it has as yet gone unchallenged and unchanged in the realm of contemporary academics.

George G. Cameron explains in his foreword to Edward Chiera's "*They Wrote on Clay*" (1938):

> "Few there are indeed who know that the name of our science, 'Assyriology' is based on an accident—the fact that the first large group of texts ever discovered were written in Assyrian. Assyrian itself is but one dialect."

Misapplication arises with use of the term to denote study of any and all ancient cuneiform-using cultures. Mardukites do not propagate this blatant disregard for the political and spiritual history of Mesopotamia. Although cuneiform-literate and sharing a similar "Anunnaki" tradition (explained further in "*Liber-51*"), Assyrians were actually northwestern foreigners to Babylon—meaning, the two are not the same. It would be just as inaccurate to refer to the study of *all* African cultures as "Egyptology."

As previously mentioned, any true esoteric analysis or mystical application are absent from the earliest academic-archaeological pursuits. These efforts mainly emphasized the *recovery* and *accumulation* of translatable materials, much of which are not yet coherently transliterated into English language even a century after their discovery. Most materials readily available to modern *Seekers* outside of the *Mardukite* brand of research and development are severely fragmented and based on other confused paradigms.

Earliest attempts at understanding ancient Mesopotamia made by "Assyriologists" of the late 19th and 20th century, included such as: E.A. Budge, Edward Chiera, L.W. King, S.L. Noah Kramer, Franqois Lenormant, R.C. Thompson and L.A. Waddell. Their renderings have already received long-standing public attention for those who sought it. The variegated cultural influences and often violent history of *Babylonia* has left a confusion of various names, titles and images that have required over a century to flush out to any practical ends, by scholars and mystics alike.

Origins for the field-name of "*Assyriology*" are derived from French excavations at the city ruins of *Khorsabad*, *Nimrud*, *Nineveh*, *Sippar* and *Lagash* (*Telloh*) in the 1840's. However, a true scientific pursuit was ignited when the royal library archives of the Assyrian king *Assurbanipal* were discovered. Thousands of clues, in the form of cuneiform tablet writings, illuminated a prehistoric legacy formerly thought of as completely forgotten and never again salvageable.

But, then, in the 1880's,

German archaeologists unearthed *Babylon...*

MARDUKITE

ZUISM

A BRIEF
INTRODUCTION

*According to the most ancient
historical records
written at the birth of our
modern civilization...* *

432,000 YEARS AGO...*

a small population of advanced beings—called the <u>ANUNNAKI</u>—began developing the planet Earth for their purposes. These elite Self-Actualized spiritual beings resided on Earth in physical bodies, but found their forms inadequate for the physical labors required. Enter: the "Human Condition." Ancient "<u>cuneiform</u>" tablet writings from Sumerians and Babylonians of Mesopotamia are clear regarding the original creation and systematic programming of Humanity.

CUNEIFORM...

is the oldest known writing system used by scribes of ancient Babylon to record their wisdom and the history of humanity on <u>clay tablets</u>. "Cuneiform" is named for its style of wedge-shaped script formed by a <u>reed pen</u> called a "<u>stylus</u>." Rather than an alphabet of letters, cuneiform is a system of "<u>signs</u>" representing "things" and "ideas." These may be combined to represent even more complex "signs."

* Version 1.1 – First published in 2019 as "*Mardukite Zuism: A Brief Introduction*" in booklet form.

Many concepts adopted for modern "Mardukite Zuism" are derived from cuneiform tablets. The ANUNNAKI introduced complex writing systems in order to program civilization and all parameters of Reality for the Human Condition. Legendary "Tablets of Destiny" (Divine Truth, supreme knowledge and cosmic power of the "gods") were first introduced to Humanity in the Babylonian narrative known best as the "Epic of Creation.

THE ARCANE TABLETS.

Ancient Babylonians used the Tablets of Destiny & Creation Epic to systematize all cosmic knowledge into a workable paradigm called "Mardukite Zuism"—a systemology received directly from the ANUNNAKI.

Paradigm : an all-encompassing standard or religion used to view the world and communicate reality.

Systemology : applied philosophies of Mardukite Zuism combined with personal spiritual techniques and technology ("Tech") that is effectively demonstrating systematic principles of a "paradigm."

THE EPIC OF CREATION.

Seven cuneiform tablets compose the ancient Babylonian Epic of Creation, named the Enuma Eliš by scholars after its opening lines. These seven tablets are the basis for what later traditions refer to as the "*Seven Days of Creation.*" The *Epic of Creation* tablets describe development of all existences with a Divine artistic perfection. The Enuma Eliš is the core example of religious literature from Babylon, which served as the basis for ancient "*Mardukite Zuism*"—the first true systematized religion in history.

THE SYSTEMOLOGY OF LIFE, UNIVERSES & EVERYTHING.

The *Arcane Tablets* describe the division of the ALL by the LAW, outside of which is but IN-FINITY. The *Epic of Creation* describes these activities as "mythology."

The Mardukite Systemology "Standard Model" uses the same information to demonstrates...

that <u>ALL</u> ("AN-KI") envelops both:
the <u>Spiritual Existences</u> ("AN")
and the <u>Physical Existences</u> ("KI")
divided by <u>Cosmic Law</u> and
connected by <u>Life-Awareness</u> ("ZU")
and beyond which is only the <u>Abyss</u>,
an <u>Infinity of Nothingness</u> ("ABZU").

ANCIENT SUMERIAN DEFINITIONS.

<u>ABZU</u> = "Abyss" ("Nothingness")
<u>ZU</u> = "Spiritual Life" ("Awareness")
<u>ANKI</u> = "All Existences" ("Existence")
<u>AN</u> = "Spiritual Universe" ("Heaven")
<u>KI</u> = "Physical Universe" ("Earth")

ALTERNATE MARDUKITE NEXGEN
SYSTEMOLOGY DEFINITIONS.

<u>ABZU</u> = "Infinity of Nothingness"
<u>ZU</u> = "Awareness of Alpha Spirit"
<u>ANKI</u> = "The Standard Model"
<u>AN</u> = "Alpha Existence" ("Spiritual")
<u>KI</u> = "Beta Existence" ("Physical")

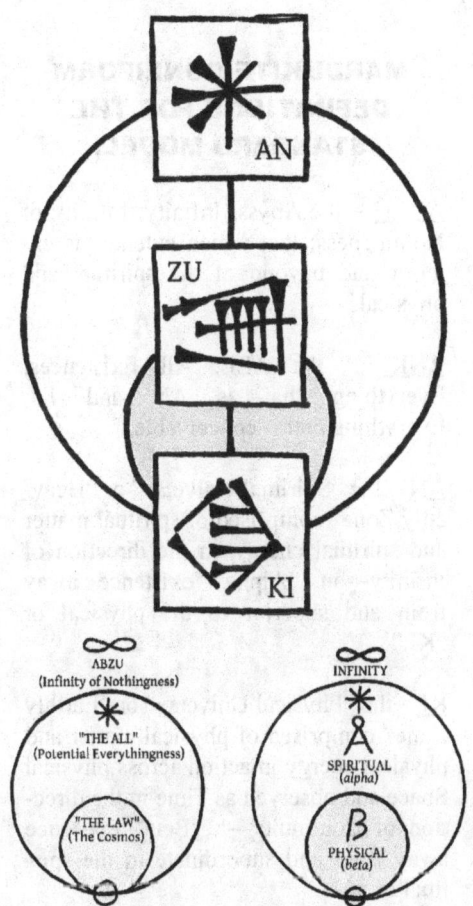

AN

ZU

KI

∞
ABZU
(Infinity of Nothingness)

"THE ALL"
(Potential Everythingness)

"THE LAW"
(The Cosmos)

∞
INFINITY

SPIRITUAL
(alpha)

PHYSICAL
(beta)

MARDUKITE CUNEIFORM DEFINITIONS FOR THE STANDARD MODEL.

<u>ABZU</u> = the Abyss; Infinity; Infinity of Nothingness; that which extends, is exterior and beyond of the spiritual and physical.

<u>ANKI</u> = the ALL; All Existences; Everything that is AN and KI; Everything that is conceivable.

<u>AN</u> = the "Spiritual Universe" or "Heavenly Zone" comprised of spiritual matter and spiritual energy, in the direction of Infinity—an "Alpha" existence away from and superior to the physical or "KI."

<u>KI</u> = the "Physical Universe" or "Earthly Zone" comprised of physical matter and physical energy in action across physical Space and observed as Time in the direction of Continuity—a "Beta" existence away from and subordinate to the spiritual or "AN."

<u>ZU</u> = "to know"; "knowingness";
"Awareness" or "consciousness"; spiritual energy and matter of AN that is
observed as "Lifeforce" in KI; "Spiritual
Life Energy"; the actual personal spiritual Identity or "Awareness" of Self as
Spirit which extends along a "line" from
the Spiritual Universe (AN) to the Physical Universe (KI).

THE TABLETS OF DESTINY &
BABYLONIAN CREATION EPIC.

The Absolute behind ALL Existence is referred
to on the *Tablets of Destiny* as the Infinity of
Nothingness. It is the only constant static of lat-
ent unmanifest potentiality of ALL and
Everythingness.

The LAW—Cosmic Law—is defined as the
Cosmic Dragon—TIAMAT—on "Epic of Creation" Tablets. She is the First Cause or
movement across a "Sea of Infinity." Later, the
LAW becomes a division between Spiritual Existence ("AN") and any Physical Universe
("KI"). The LAW—Tiamat—permeating ALL,
uses the *Tablets of Destiny* and then fixes the

systems of finite potential: The Systems of Manifestation—Substance, Motion and Awareness.

"Before heaven or earth are named," the formation and interaction of active existences —"substances" and "bodies" and "Life" and "gods"—creates turbulence and waves of action through space. The governing system of Cosmic Law—Tiamat—responds accordingly. She fixes the Tablets of Destiny to her "deputy"—a messenger wave action of the LAW named "Kingu" and sends him rippling out to "meet" the Anunnaki "gods."

The Anunnaki Assembly of "gods" prepare to battle The LAW. When none among them comes forth to engage, it is the Anunnaki "god" MARDUK that volunteers as hero to confront Kingu and Tiamat—but with a condition that the Anunnaki Assembly recognize him as "Chief of the Gods" upon his success.

When MARDUK approaches the LAW directly, he is flanked by Kingu and the "army of Ancient Ones." MARDUK is able to relinquish the Tablets of Destiny from Kingu. With the Tablets of Destiny, Marduk conquers a true understanding of Cosmic Law and thereby Tiamat.

THE TABLETS OF DESTINY
& SELF-HONESTY.

Marduk uses the Tablets of Destiny to discover "Self-Honesty" and Divine Knowledge governing "Cosmic Ordering"—systems dividing the "Spiritual Universe" (AN) from a "Physical Universe" (KI). The two universes are connected only by a stream of Spiritual Lifeforce Awareness that Sumerians called ZU. Wisdom from the Arcane Tablets is later passed down to and concealed by an ancient esoteric secret society in Babylon: the Scribes, High Priests and Priestesses of Mardukite Zuism.

Self-Honesty is a term describing an original "Alpha" state of clear knowingness and Self-directed beingness."Self-Honesty" is the most basic and true expression of Self as "I-AM"—free of artificial attachments; reactive-response conditioning; and imposed or enforced programming as Reality for the Human Condition. Spiritual development in modern *Mardukite Zuism* is referred to as the "Pathway to Self-Honesty" and the "Gateway to Infinity." It is modeled directly from the Ancient Mystery Tradition observed at the Temples of Babylon.

THE KEY TO THE GATE.

"I will take my Blood—and with Bone—I will fashion a Race of Humans to keep Watch of the Gate. And from the Blood of Kingu I will create another Race of Humans to inhabit the Earth in service to the Gods—so shrines to the Anunnaki may be built and the temples filled. I will bind the Elder Gods to the Watchtowers; let them keep watch over the Gate of Abzu and the Gate of Tiamat and Gate of Kingu—and with a Key that shall be ever hidden, known to none, except only to my Mardukites." —MARDUK, *Enuma Elis, Creation Tablet VI*.

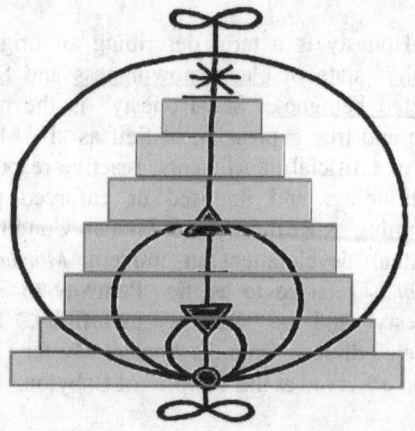

THE ANUNNAKI LADDER OF LIGHTS & BABYLONIAN GATEWAYS TO INFINITY.

ZIGGURAT TEMPLES in Babylonia—and throughout Mesopotamia—served to remind populations of the ZU connecting "Heaven" and "Earth."

Seven-stepped "levels" of the physical ZIG-GURAT TEMPLES of Babylonia—and seven corresponding Gates—represent spiritual levels of actualized Awareness; states of Self-purification (or "spiritual defragmentation") as they ascend in the direction of AN toward Infinity of Supreme Beingness—the Pathway of Self-Honesty—in imitation of the footsteps of the gods during their descent through the "spheres" or "Gates."

COSMOLOGY AND METAPHYSICS.

All Things in the Physical Universe are in motion—wave motions of "energy and matter in space measured as-and-across time." Continuity of the Physical Universe (KI) is divided by LAW and encompassed by the ALL (ANKI).

The direction of AN extends toward ABZU, an Infinity of Nothingness beyond effective existence.

The true <u>Alpha Self</u> is a source—the "spiritual cause" of "physical effects." It engages a <u>Self-determined WILL</u> from its "spiritual" <u>Alpha existence</u> to actualize Awareness for "physical" <u>Beta existence</u> experience as "Life."

USING ANCIENT WISDOM TO UNLOCK HUMAN POTENTIAL.

Communication of clear wisdom and true knowledge from Arcane Tablets is distorted as it passes through time and geography, diverse languages and authoritarian cultures using the "Power" to program the masses and fragment the Human Condition away from Self-Honesty.

Use of this ancient wisdom reveals the Keys to "<u>Cosmic Ordering</u>"—applying the highest Self-directed understanding of "cause-and-effect" sequences in the Physical Universe.

MARDUKITE ZUISM, SYSTEMOLOGY & SPIRITUALITY.

The Spiritual Universe (AN)—of metaphysical or spiritual energy and metaphysical or spiritual matter is not dependent on the Physical Universe (KI) to exist; the two are existentially independent of each other, maintaining a single channel, conduit or connection, which is <u>Alpha Spirit</u> "Awareness" as Spiritual Life or ZU. The Alpha Spirit engages a <u>ZU-line</u>, a spiritual lifeline of ZU energy to a genetic vehicle or organic body to experience physical beta existence.

MARDUKITE ZUISM DEFINITIONS FOR SYSTEMOLOGY.

<u>ALPHA SPIRIT</u> = a spiritual lifeform; the True Self or "I-AM"; the spirit that is controlling the physical body or "genetic vehicle" using a Lifeline or continuum of spiritual "ZU" energy.

<u>ASCENSION</u> = actualized Awareness elevated to (AN) spiritual existence that is exterior to beta-existence.

BETA-EXISTENCE = manifestation in the Physical Universe (KI); the state of existence or condition of frequency specific to physical energy and physical matter in physical space.

FRAGMENTATION = breaking into parts; fractioning wholeness; fracture of holism; discontinuity; separation; outside the state of Self-Honesty.

GENETIC VEHICLE = a physical life-form; the physical (beta) body controlled by the (Alpha) Spirit using a continuous Lifeline of ZU energy.

HUMAN CONDITION = a default programmed conditioned state standard issue Human existence/experience.

ZU-LINE = a spectrum of Spiritual Life-Energy (ZU); an energetic channel or Identity-Continuum connecting Alpha Spirit Awareness from Infinity-to-Infinity including the full physical beta range.

THE HIGHEST FORM OF
TRUE DIVINE WORSHIP.

The true Destiny of Humanity is to achieve spiritual <u>Self-Actualization</u>; the reunion of Self with the Divine. Attaining Self-Honesty in this Life is the most important step a person can take toward achieving their highest ideals, goals and realizations.

The Highest form of "True Worship" begins with the Spirit—the true Self—and all external practices, rituals, ceremonies and historical examples are but outer reflections of this ideal. The Highest form of "Sin" is against the Spirit —against the Self—and its ability to maintain Self-Honesty. There are modes of thought, action and Self-direction of effort that will contribute toward Ascension; and modes that lead away from that.

Beta experiences of "Sin"—pain, fear, guilt, anger—are all related to personal fragmentation; and emotional turbulence from all of these may be released—and intention energy redirected— because: <u>we are all co-creators of Reality in this lifetime!</u>

SPHERES OF EXISTENCE, INFLUENCE & UTILITARIAN ETHICS OF SYSTEMOLOGY.

The prime directive of all beta existence is: *to exist*. The continuation of existence is the purpose behind all existence. Between realization of Self and Infinity, there are many spheres of existence that we may influence. All of the spheres are interconnected.

There is nothing in existence that is in absolute exclusion to all existence. Each sphere of existence supports subsequent existences and assists reaches toward higher spheres of influence.

The greatest good contributes to the greatest continuation of optimum existence for the greatest sphere of inclusion. Degrees of rightness and wrongness are determined by Cosmic Law and are reflected in the quality of, and continuation of, an optimal existence at the highest sphere of existence.

Individual happiness is attained via the channel to the highest sphere. Human unhappiness is the result of "selfishness" and/or lack of "spiritual Self-Actualization" and "Awareness."

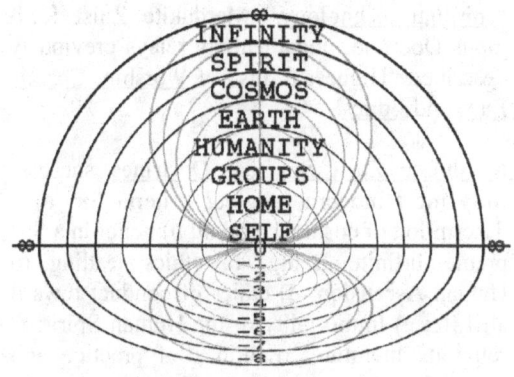

ZU : MARDUKITE ZUISM &
MODERN ZUIST RELIGION.

History demonstrates how dangerous, trouble-
some and easily misused the concept of "REL-
GION" is; so, for purposes of incorporating
Mardukite Zuism as a contemporary standard,
the idea of "religion" is here treated as:

a concise spiritual paradigm, set of beliefs and practices, regarding Divinity,
Infinite Beingness—or else "God."

Mardukite Zuism operates under a premise of
very specific beliefs and a "systemology" of

"spiritual technology." Mardukite Zuist Religious Doctrine fundamentally relays previously described "Highest forms" of Worship, Cosmic Law, and Ethics.

Mardukite Zuist Spiritual Doctrines successfully meet modern religious criteria for: a) a description of cosmic creation; b) belief in a Supreme Infinite Being; c) ethics leading to Human Ascension; d) ethics of conduct toward all Life; e) Immortality of the Human Spirit; f) religious literature, traditions of practice and spiritual advisement.

GOALS & IDEALS OF MARDUKITE ZUISM.

The word "ZU" meant "knowing" in original Sumerian cuneiform script. Goals and ideals of Zuism reflect this. Mardukite Zuism seeks to assist an individual in reclaiming a realization of the True Self or "I-AM" as the Immortal Spirit, in line with a most ancient directive: to "Know Thyself."

In view of the fact that all modern humans are subjected to technologies depriving them of their freedoms to *be*, *think*, *know* and pursue truth: the goals and ideals of Zuism are to effectively revive and repair these very abilities and certainties of the Individual—as an increase of "Actualized Awareness."

INFINITY, "GOD" &
SUPREME BEINGNESS

The Spiritual Philosophy of Zuism is systematized by a Standard Model. It demonstrates Absolute Supreme Beingness associated with the Highest realization of "God" as INFINITY. No thing is Higher or Absolute than the Infinity of Nothing—and reducing Supreme Beingness to any finite personality or character trait is to limit and defile with lesser "words."

The Highest Name of God cannot be conceived —hence our symbolic use of the Infinity Sign:

∞

...or Sumerian cuneiform word-sign: "ABZU"
—"The Infinite Nothingness and
Source of All ZU."

The Spiritual Universe (AN) is *All-as-One* because it exists as an infinite singularity or stasis:

infinite potential with no gradient or observed motion; which is its own continuity.

The Physical Universe (KI) is *All-as-One* because it is in continuous motion, with all manifest parts working systematically as a continuity of beta-existence.

A "spiritual continuum" or "conduit channel" of ZU—absolute energy from the Spiritual Universe (AN)—links our Awareness levels of "I-AM," "True Self" or Spirit ("Alpha Spirit") with the degrees of motion and variation in the Physical Universe.

This Alpha Spirit or "Soul" is the true Awareness, "I" or "Self" connected to the operation and control of the physical body.

THE TRUE HUMAN ALPHA SPIRIT.

The true Self is the "I" or "Spirit" regardless of its position, degree or level of Awareness. Spirit remains. Whatever "spiritual energy-matter" composes the Alpha Spirit or "soul"—it must occupy this "other space" with its spiritual existence and then project its Awareness and Will onto the Physical Universe (KI) in order to experience the Game we call Life.

This "spiritual energy-matter" that composes all Life (as a Lifeforce with Awareness and Consciousness) goes by many names throughout history—but we find the idea first treated as <u>ZU</u> on cuneiform tablets of Mesopotamia.

On an Identity lifeline of ZU energy, all Alpha Spirits are operating from a Spiritual Universe. We refer to this as the ZU-line on the Standard Model.

ZU is the name given to the spiritual essence of all Life in existence—and Self is a concentrated center or focal point as a ZU-continuum or Identity.

The True Self of an Individual Human is a "spiritual universe cause" of "physical universe effects"—engaging as an immortal Alpha Spirit with a Self-determined Will actualized as an Awareness along the ZU-continuum, extending from Infinity-to-Infinity, through every possible frequency and vibration along the total spectrum of physical and metaphysical existence.

THE SYSTEMOLOGY PRACTICES OF SPIRITUAL ADVISEMENT & COUNSELING SERVICES FOR MARDUKITE ZUISM.

The Mardukite Chamberlains were established in 2009 dedicated to recovery and consolidation of all historical, scriptural & ritual records of ancient Babylon in Mesopotamia. In 2011, a Mardukite faction (International Systemology Society) began to research and develop methods to apply ancient wisdom as a futurist spiritual technology that awakens, unlocks and fully actualizes spiritual potential of the Human Condition.

A systematic approach to spirituality is seen on the Standard Model, where ZU-line frequencies are represented at various degrees: "zero-point" body death; cellular activity and sensory perceptions of a genetic body; bio-chemicals induced by emotion; thoughts and intention transmitted between our Alpha Spirit and the "genetic vehicle"—all the way "up" the scale to a perfected clarity of Self-Actualized Awareness of I-AM as our true "Alpha" state, just below Infinity and Absolute Beingness.Full potential of ZU in Consciousness is only altered from its natural state as a result of personal fragmentation of the Human Condition. This may be restored with spiritual practices.

The Pathway to Self-Honesty is a personal journey and spiritual adventure marked by progressive clearing of spiritual energy channels fragmented by the imprinting and programming accumulated from experiences in our environment—the "debris" that fragments the total actualized experience of Self in Awareness as the Alpha Spirit.

The first and most important step—Before an individual can actualize potentials of the Spirit as Self, they must fully realize: the I-AM Self and the Alpha Spirit are One.

This state of Knowingness is the primary intention of basic spiritual practices found in Mardukite Zuism.

"Systemology" books and advanced training courses are also available to Mardukite Ministers seeking to qualify as specialized clergy, priests, priestess, and systematic processing pilots.

CREED OF MARDUKITE ZUISM.
PRINCIPLES OF BELIEF.*

1.) We believe in an Absolute Beingness, which is Infinite—the ABZU—the All-as-One encompassing Source of All Being, Knowing and Awareness to all Alpha (Spiritual-AN) and Beta (Physical-KI) states of existence.

2.) We believe in a spiritual energy of all Life and Awareness—ZU—in the physical universe (beta) that is an effect of a spiritual (Alpha) cause; a Spirit that is cause. This Spirit—in its Alpha state—is the True Self "I-AM" Individual Identity that many have called the "soul."

3.) We believe that the Human Condition is a genetic vehicle used by a spiritual source (AN) to experience the Finite as physical existence (KI)—that we are Awareness (ZU) projected onto a genetic vehicle—and that while the vehicle/body may perish to physical entropy, the "Alpha Spirit" remains immortal and Self-directed to the extent of its own Actualized Awareness.

---

* First drafted in 2019.

4.) We believe that the highest form of worship and spirituality is the actualization and advancement of our "Self" as Spirit in Self-Honesty—and that Self-Honesty is the I-AM Alpha state of Being and Knowing, which is realizable in this lifetime.

5.) We believe that the purpose of all existence is: to exist—and that the prime directive of all spiritual Life is: continued existence of spiritual Life and co-creation of habitable Reality. "Good" and "Moral" actions are evaluated to the extent of this end.

6A.) We believe that no Life exists in exclusion to all other Life—and that the conditions of a habitable Reality extending from Self include:
Home; Community; All Humanity; All Life on Earth; All Life in the Universe; All Spiritual Life; and the Infinite.

6B.) We believe in a continued evolution of Alpha Spirit awareness developed beyond one physical life, and that a Spirit experiences many.

7A.) We believe Mardukite Zuism and its applied systemology is a 21st Century AD synthesis of the 21st Century BC wisdom collected on cuneiform tablets and experienced in ancient Mesopotamia, esp. Babylon.

7B.) This cuneiform library included details concerning: beings called the Anunnaki; ordering of the Cosmos; creation of Humanity; and an entire legacy of systematized traditions.

8.) We believe in the continuation of, and proper communication of, the true legacy of Human history—and the ability of every Human to realize that they are a Free Spirit in a Free Zone of Self-Determinism: and no "evils" can affect intentions if an individual is spiritually Self-Actualized in Self-Honesty.

THE ARCANE KNOWLEDGE FROM MARDUK'S TABLET OF DESTINY.*

1.) As above, so below;
On earth as it is in Heaven
an-bala ki-bala an-ba ki an-ba

2.) What the Mind believes, the Spirit reinforces
da-ga nam-ku-zu dingir-Lamma a bi-ib-gar

3.) When disaster is self-made,
no man can interfere
*nig-ku-lam-ma dingir-ra-na-ka su—
tu-tu nu-ub-zu*

4.) What is given in submission
is a catalyst for defiance
nig-gu-gar-ra nig-gaba-gar-ra

5.) Whoever partners with Truth, creates Life
nig-ge-na-ta a-ba in-da-di nam-ti i-u-tu

---

* From *"Tablets of Destiny (Revelation)"* by Joshua Free.

Before Babylon...

When history had not yet been written...

ANUNNAKI HISTORY &

MAGIC

MARDUKITE LIBER-51

— 1 —
MESOPOTAMIAN MYSTERIES
Before Babylon and the Land of Sumer

*"Here [in Babylon] is real death. Not a column
or arch still stands to demonstrate the
permanency of human work. Everything has
crumbled to dust. The very temple tower, the
most imposing of all these ancient
constructions, has entirely lost its shape.
Where are now its seven stages? We see nothing
but a mound of earth – all that remains of the
millions of its bricks. Here the ancient mysteries
and their tombs have been sleeping quietly for
millenniums. In a few months, perhaps in a few
days, the ground will be broken by trenches as
in a battlefield. And the repose of the poor dead
will be disturbed by the frantic search for
records and data..."*

~ Edward Chiera, *From a letter to his wife.*

Before Babylon—when history had not yet been
written—lands now known as the Middle East
were first occupied by "gods" and "demi-gods"
of antiquity—the *Anunnaki*. These super-human
figures molded and shaped human consciousness and the systematized civilization we so
easily take for granted in the "Western World"

today. The wheel of time forced the age of "gods" to become an era of "men" and *their* ways, but ancient foundations built and established in Mesopotamia remain strong and alive among us today.

Classical period Greeks may be credited with the term: *Mesopotamia*—meaning "A land between two rivers." More literal than poetic, the title accurately describes the region also once known to the ancients as *Babylonia*—the "Land of the Gates of the Gods" and "City of Star-Gates" established primarily between two rivers—the *Tigris* and the *Euphrates*. Today, the term *Babylonia* is often used politically to distinguish post-Sumerian *empires* in Mesopotamia, maintained by *Babylonian* kings—a lineage made famous by Hammurabi, a powerful civic *systematizer* of Mardukite Babylon.

Commonly compared to the fertile Nile region of Egypt, *Mesopotamia* is also a river-delta system—and, like the Nile to the Egyptians, this system of life-giving waters proved to be inseparable from prosperity of the people. The plain was cultivated successfully by use of the first "aqueduct-irrigation" systems. Accurate construction and upkeep of these canals were vital to keep *Babylonia* habitable in all seasons. Eventually, as they were abandoned under foreign control, dissolution of the aqueduct system resulted in complete collapse of *Babylon* as the "throne of the earth" and its nation returned to the indistinct sand it once emerged from.

Ancient Mesopotamia is famous for its original inhabitants—those who occupied the area before, and reestablished it after, a "Great Flood"—"Uruk Sumerians" and "Akkadian Babylonians" (and later "Assyrians"); indigenous folk calling their native land *kengir*—meaning "local." The proto-Sumerian "Ubaid" launched the first primary post-diluvian Mesopotamian cities: *Eridu, Ur, Isin, Larsa, Lagash, Nippur* and *Uruk* (also known as *Erech* and possibly the origins of the name *Iraq*), all positioned on established structural foundations from a former age.

Charting exact political boundaries of *Babylonia* is difficult. They are not generally agreed upon—no more today among scholars and nationalists then by those who once physically fought for them in periods of antiquity. For as long as humans have been involved, the area has been plagued with constant conflict. Mesopotamian territory and reign often included areas well beyond the pathway of the two rivers, which even themselves changed in the positions of their course over time due to thousands of years of alteration (then absence) by Anunnaki (then human) intervention.

Ancient *Babylonia* essentially occupies present-day Iraq, in a region bordered by mountains separating it (on the east) from Iran; ancient Persia. To the south, the empire once extended to the Persian Gulf where the archetypal city of *Eridu* was founded. On the western front, Mesopotamia is separated from the Mediterranean and Magan lands, Egypt (or Khem), by the vast expanse of Arabian desert, and just north of this: the land of Syria.

The full expanse of the "Ancient Near East" includes geographical locations now occupied as Iran, Iraq, Saudi Arabia, Yemen, Oman, Lebanon, Israel, Syria and the United Arab Emirates. Mesopotamian kingdoms also included (at some time or another) occupations in modern-day Turkey, Armenia, Afghanistan, Pakistan, Egypt and Sudan. The modern term "Middle East" is a Euro-centric political semantic replacing academic usage of the "Near East," as opposed to the "Far East" or "oriental." With few exceptions, the Ancient Near East and its *Anunnaki* legacy is the direct origin of most major world religions in history, including (but not limited to): Zoroastrianism (Mazdaism), Mithraism, Yezidism (Yazdanism), Manichaeism, Canaanite, Baha'i, Islam, Judaism and Christianity.

The legendary city of Babylon stood alongside the western-laying of the two rivers, the *Euphrates* (in Greek) called *burannon* or *perath* by Sumerians (and *puratu* by Assyrians)—all meaning simply "river." It is considerably longer of the two rivers—at 1,800 miles—forming first in the heights of the mountains at 11,000 feet above sea level. It quickly drops off then falls approximately one foot per mile for the last 1,200 miles of its run. The river path has consistently moved westward with absence of human intervention and canals—creating more area "between" the rivers. The water levels are indicative of equinoxes, like the Egyptian Nile, with the *Euphrates* rising in the spring and lowering in the autumn. Although unlike the Nile, which is altered by the summer monsoon season, the water levels of the *Euphrates* river peaks in the springtime.

Opposite the *Euphrates*, the broad eastern river runs 1,150 miles and, like the other, the path has also shifted to what archeologists believe to be its more 'natural' flow with the abandonment of the irrigation canals. Greeks pronounced the Assyrian river name as *Tigris*, essentially meaning "*serpent river*" (*i-di-ik-lat*), though its original Sumerian identification meant "*fast as an arr-*

ow" (*idigna* or *id-dagal-la*). Babylonians found the *Tigris* to be too wild to cross easily or irrigate with. The water levels also rise and fall in direct opposition to the cycle of the *Euphrates*. Ancient cities founded alongside (and making use of) the *Tigris River* include *Nineveh, Calah (Nimrud)* and *Asshur*. Before emptying into the Persian Gulf, the *Euphrates* and *Tigris* join together forming a marshy delta region called the "Great Swamp." The prehistoric city of *Eridu* was once a lavish capital there, at the coast of the Persian Gulf. Today, however, ruins and remains of *Eridu* now rest 130 miles away from the sea. This shift over time is attributed to a "shrinking" Persian Gulf, creating more land—approximately *72 feet* of it *per* year!

"E-RI-DU" [*House in the Distance, Built*] is the original Mesopotamian home of the Anunnaki god *Enki*—a prototype-city of *Babylon* built prior to the "Great Flood," later rebuilt, ever remaining the sacred precinct of *Enki* in *Babylonia*. It is the oldest capital city of the Ubaid (proto-Uruk) Sumerians, dated to over seven-thousand years ago. Its remains are found at *Tell abu Shahrain* (Arabic name). In *Eridu*, the modern practices of "ceremonial" and religious "magic" (or "magick" if you prefer) were born. The Anunnaki god *Marduk* and his demigod son

Nabu apprenticed there, learning not only esoteric spiritual arts, but many other intellectual (or "divine") sciences governed by *Enki*.

Ubaid-Sumerians (or proto-Sumerians) occupied Mesopotamia before the Uruk-Sumerians, the origins of what we historically consider "Enlilite Sumerians"—from at least the Fifth Millennium B.C. The designated name of "*Ubaid*" comes only from modern archaeological excavation of ruins at *Tell Ubaid*—a primitive city built near the area later established as the Uruk-Sumerian city of Ur. True urban systematization became present during Uruk occupation and was later perfected by the Babylonians, who inspired Empire-builders forever thereafter.

Distinct natural terrain separate Mesopotamia into northern and southern parts; a factor long exploited for political purposes to define boundaries. Originally, southern *Sumer* (Also called *Sumeria*, *Shinar*, *Babili*, *Babylonia* or *Chaldea* in varying texts) and northern *Akkad* each were ruled by their own governors, called a *patesi*. [Modern "Mardukites" retained usage of the title to indicate a priest/minister-bishop of a particular region or diocese.] A post-Sumerian unification of the two lands and rise of the *Babylonian Empire* led to replacing this role with the *lugal*—a title applied to the "*Mighty King of both Sumer & Akkad*"—Literally: *lu*—man; *gal* —great or lofty. The "Big Man"—*The King*.

The northern half of Mesopotamia was once forested and so it retains features of prairie and plains mixed with a mountainous supply of stones and crystals. The southern part is naturally more barren, primarily swamps and marshes mixed with arid desert. Without the aid of an incredible irrigation system, the *Babylonian Empire* would never have had the freedom and sustainability to survive and flourish as the spiritual and political epicenter of the ancient world.

The ever-changing shape of the land was once expertly engineered to meet needs of an awe-inspiring unparalleled civilization. Proper cultivation of the land was the original key—making societal life possible among humans, and of this knowledge they attributed to the *gods*—great beings who taught the people how to survive, and then to thrive, launching domestic urban city-life to sustain a continued existence on earth.

With the 'land between the rivers' prepared and consecrated, *kingship* could now be *lowered* from *heaven*...

— 2 —

SARGON & THE SUMERIANS
Divine Right and the Land of Sumer

*An examination of the Sumerian and Babyloni-
an King-Lists will reveal the belief that "kingship" was "sent down" from "heaven" as decreed by the gods. To this we might add that a
similar tradition has been followed by many indigenous ancient cultures. These dynastic lists
originate by Sumerian hands, but were later re-
catalogued in Babylon by Nabu Priest-Scribes.
Similar King-Lists have also been found in
Egypt and they all suggest some very amazing
notions for the contemporary mind to grasp.*

~ Joshua Free, *original Liber-51 Lecture*

"Divine Right" to reign on earth "lowered
down" from the "heavens" to *Eridu*—but "kingship" moved around quite a bit. Prior to establishment of *Mardukite Babylon*, most Uruk-Sumerian activity concentrated in southern
parts of Mesopotamia. *Eridu*—home of *Enki*—
becomes a secondary capital when Sumerian
cultural and "religious" emphasis develops in
the *Enlilite* city of *Uruk* (also called *Erech*).

To establish *Uruk* as a capital *holy city* in the

consciousness of Sumerians, the national sacred *ziggurat* temple-shrine of *Anu*—the E-ANNA—was built there to accommodate rare appearances made by the highest *Anunnaki* Divine Couple—*Anu* and *Antu*—on earth. This *ziggurat* was later "gifted" to the Anunnaki goddess *Inanna-Ishtar*, from which she based her own worldly rule.

Kingship is a central function to establishing "societal systems," forming the basis of Sumerian and Babylonian lore—and all later paradigms directly born from the Anunnaki (traditions). Examination of ancient *King-Lists* from Mesopotamia echo the oldest, archaic, premise that "kingship" was *brought down*—or *sent down* from the "heavens"—as decreed by, and representative of, the gods. But, of course, the idea of *monarchy* or kingship was not always executed by humans to the highest regard—or in *Self-Honesty*; misuse of these systems always leads to their inevitable breakdown. The complete text of the cuneiform *King-Lists* is found as the *Mardukite Tablet-K* Series.* The oldest example in Sumerian language is the *Weld-Blundell Prism*. These records were later adapted and

---

* Refer to "*The Complete Anunnaki Bible*" or "*The Anunnaki Bible: New Standard Zuist Edition*" edited by Joshua Free.

preserved by Babylonian scribes, then again by the classical Historian Berossus in the 3rd Century B.C. A similar chronicle was prepared around the same time for Egyptian libraries by the Historian Manetho.

Linear chronology of the *King-Lists* are separated by a critical event, one found in cosmological records of most ancient cultures—the *Deluge* or *Great Flood*. This means that Sumerian civilization actually began in *antediluvian* times, prior to the *Deluge*. The *King-Lists* are consistent with this time scale too, but the shifting sands of Mesopotamia provide us few direct clues. Ancient sites were often dismantled or found in ruins and later built over by cultural successors. What this signifies is that pre-Babylonian, pre-Sumerian *Ubaid* periods are not absolute origins for this prehistoric civilization, but instead are origins for efforts resumed after the earth was stable for societal habitation again, possibly following the last Ice Age.

Ancient writings do not actually dispute that pre-Sumerian "civilizations" and other Anunnaki "experiments" have come and gone on the planet. Archeologists can successfully confirm identities of the *King-Lists* until c. 3200 B.C., and yet these records continue for nearly another 430,000 years into the past.

Sumerian and Egyptian records are very clear about the nature of the beings occupying seats of kingship at its inception—*gods*. Original *overseers* were considered *divine*, thought to have come from the stars/sky and bringing with them the knowledge and technologies that could cultivate humanity. Reign of these *divine* beings was eventually replaced by *hybrid demigods* (part-*Divine*; part-*human*) until finally passed to control of a specialized segment—*Royal Blood* —of mankind. Hybrid offspring of gods as kings were *demigods*, which required both parents to be 'divine', but the offspring could be born on earth. "Part-" or "half-" divine 'kings' later emerging in the population required only one 'divine' or 'demigod' parent.

LIFESPANS ON THE KING-LISTS

"Divine" = *10,000's* of years old
"Demigod" = *1,000's* of years old
"Deity/Hero" = *100's* of yeas old

god + god = demigod ("*divine*")
demigod + god = demigod ("*lordly*")
god + human = deity ("*half-divine*")
demigod + human = deity ("*half-divine*")
deity + human = hero ("*quarter-breed*")

At each stage of development, the concept of *dynastic succession* remains paramount—the idea that "Divine Blood" flows from the heart of *true* kings in the lineage, which in turn may be passed on to their offspring. The tradition of *Divine Right to Rule* is as ancient as human society altogether and may even have origins beyond only this planet. Cosmological tablets illuminate a similar tradition of *Divine Succession* practiced by the *Anunnaki* ("sky gods")—particularly *Anu, Enlil* and *Enki*—describing control of heavenly domains and celestial zones.

Origins for the word "ruler," "regent" and "realm" all reflect the perceived "god-like" nature of the original "King" role. After the unification of the two lands of Mesopotamia, one hero-man—one *lugal*—was elevated to the position of a blessed and lofty *demigod.* More than simply a title of power, this role required the person to be an active intermediary between the people and the *gods* and thus acted as a powerful *priest-king*.

Interconnectedness between the "realm" and the king was inseparable. The king and his land are one. The king and his people are one. The fate of one has proved to reflect in the other throughout history and populations couldn't deny observing it—a good and just king resulted in social expansion and a fruitful land, whereas rule of unjust ungodly tyrants weakened the integrity of the *Babylonian Empire* every time.

Properly guided kings realized they were essentially a *Divine Representation* on earth and with this came great responsibility. In fact, the freedoms, responsibilities and penalties of Mesopotamian society all *rose* relative with class—quite different even, than what we see often today. The 'true' kings understood that they existed *for* the people, representatives of the *gods* on earth, exercising a *divine power* reflecting the *gods* themselves during the cultivation of the "human condition."

Descent of kingship came from the *gods of heaven* themselves, but is carried in the hearts of men—passed on as genetic memory. Recognition of "Divine Blood" conjured a system known as "*jure divino*"—the episcopal law (from the Greek *episkopos*, meaning "overseer") upheld by an individual "anointed" or "chosen" by *God*.

> *"I am Sargon, the Mighty King of Akkad.*
> *Marduk smiled upon me,*
> *And by his love,*
> *I was made a ruler of the kingdom."*

Sargon of Akkad (*Sharru-Kin*)—also called Sargon-the-Great—is sometimes confused by amateur researchers with another later Babylonian king sharing the same name, Sargon II, an Assyrian who appears on the scene nearly two-thousand years afterward during the *Neo-Babylonian Empire*.

Sargon is the first "Babylonian" King to reign supreme over all of the lands in Mesopotamia. He is founder of the Akkadian dynasty and the archetypal World Emperor, but was also the first *Mardukite King*—a chosen chamberlain, blessed by the Anunnaki god *Marduk*, patron deity of *Babylon*. A chaotic anti-Sumerian hold on the land by a pre-Babylonian tribe called the Umma was relinquished in c. 2600 B.C. by Sargon. [Although texts developed by scribes of Nabunidus—providing a academically rejected count known as the "long chronology"—indicate this time as c. 3750 BC.]

Similar to the story of Moses, Sargon is the bastard son of a priestess. He is placed in a reed basket and floated down a river, found, then raised by the *King of Kish*. He grows up to overthrow the king and declares himself supreme in *Akkad* and then setting his sights on *Sumer*—the campaign for a southern Mesopotamian take-over ensues, beginning with the city of *Uruk*.

His sophisticated military operations coupled with a weights and measures standardization allowed unified organization of the first "world empire."

Sargon's son Rimush (c. 2580 B.C.) reigned after his father's death, becoming the self-proclaimed *King of Kish*—a title which cost him his life. After his murder, his brother Manishtusu replaced him, during which another tribe, the Elamites, revolt. His son, Naram-Sin, named himself the *King of the Four Quarters* and successfully conquered the Magan lands located on the Arabian peninsula, separating Mesopotamia from Egypt. He wrongfully did so in the tradition of the Enlilite *Anunnaki gods*—rejecting his Mardukite heritage—and as punishment for supporting a neo-Sumerian Renaissance, the rapid expansion caused the heart of a once-Mardukite global empire to weaken...at least, *for a time*.

— 3 —

SIFTING THE SUMERIAN SANDS
Unearthing the Anunnaki Legacy of Kings

"Since Marduk created me to be king and Nabu has culled his people to my realm – as the love I have for my own life, so do I feel toward the building and reign of their cities."

~ King Nebuchadnezzar II, *Mardukite Tablet-L*

Sargon's Akkadian Dynasty began in northern Mesopotamia—in lands of Akkad. Akkadian territory and influence was of only tribal significance during the early rise of Sumerians proper, but when Sargon used his military to unify the "two lands" of Mesopotamia, he established the first true Sumerian empire in the world. Indeed, for the first time, the lands of *Akkad* and *Sumer* were governed from a single capital: Sargon's city of *Agade* (the city of *Akkad* in the land of *Akkad*, like *Babylon* in *Babylonia* and even *New York, New York*), a city named after the word "unity" in Akkadian language.

As a culture and language, Akkadian evolved alongside, but separate, from the southern Sumerians. It is fortunate, however, that they were participants in the same Celestial *Anunna-*

ki tradition. Akkadians possessed their own distinct proto-Semitic culture and language, but shared the Sumerian dedication to an *Anunnaki* "pantheon" and also used a refined version of cuneiform 'wedge-styled' writing to represent their own language, which replaced the Sumerian *emegir* mother-tongue. Akkadian language also evolved separately as other Semitic languages, like Hebrew, Canaanite, Phoenician, Arabic and Aramaic.

Assimilation of many pre-Babylonian (Sumerian) "programs" and Enlilite "systems" permitted a social transition into post-Sumerian or "Mardukite" ideologies. This energetic change and paradigm-shift in human consciousness occurred simultaneously as humanity entered the astrological Age of Aries in 2160 B.C. Several Sumerian literary cycles (cuneiform tablet series) are retained almost verbatim—inscribed by a new order of mystic-scribes or magician-priests using Akkadian language. For example: *Inanna-Ishtar's Descent into the Underworld* and the *Epic of Gilgamesh* are both of purely Sumerian (pre-Babylonian) origin. Versions simply remained existent in Babylonian libraries.

This new (post-Sumerian) Babylonian-Akkadian literary and religious tradition shifted emphasis from an Enlilite "World Order" to a dedication of *Marduk*. The "Mardukite Legacy" replaces the old paradigm altogether. Although the actual identities of the Supernal Trinity (*Anu*, *Enlil* and *Enki*) and Anunnaki pantheon already established remain, the emphasis turns to the "younger generation" of Anunnaki, best represented in Babylonian Tradition.

THE ANUNNAKI "SUPERNAL TRINITY"

Anu—the *distant* "Father" in *heaven* who birthed and "commanded" the Anunnaki gods visiting earth.

Enlil—the *local* "Father" in the *skies* who established the Sumerian "World Order" of the Anunnaki gods of earth.

Enki—the *patron* "Father" on *earth* who maintains all Anunnaki "systems" and cosmic "programs" of existence.

The new Babylonian vision heralded the new god *Marduk* as a local patron deity of *Babylon*. This replaced more primitive ideals and loosely organized standards of rural Sumerian life with systematized urbanization (that humans continue to live in the shadows of). All these new traditions attributed to *Marduk* and his *Babylon* were inherited from his *Anunnaki* father, *Enki*—magic and wisdom, sciences and religion; these become central icons for city and community infrastructure, temples, libraries and *ziggurats*.

In pre-Babylonian *Sumer*, *Enki* assisted his brother *Enlil* in the development of the *cosmos*—the organization of physical worldly systems (or 'world order'). *Enki* is given domain of the physical sciences, mathematics and esoteric magic. Among the "Race of Marduk" (*Mardukite Babylonians*), *Enki* is sometimes referred to as "Our Father." This arm of the Supernal Trinity is shared with his espoused consort *Ninki*, also known as *Damkina*.

By earlier Sumerian standards during the Age of Taurus (c.4200-2160 B.C.), *Enlil* is heir to "*Anuship*" in "*Heaven*"—the position of "God" for the local universe. Later duality observed in the Babylonian pantheon between lineages of *Enki* and *Enlil* occurred "on earth as it is in heaven." *Anu*, by name and title, is the "Father in Heaven," the All-Father to the *gods*—but particularly the biological parent to both *Enki* and *Enlil*.

Most of Sargon's immediate descendents did not possess his same integrity when he first conducted his world building campaign—even as militant, and as much of a warlord as he was. His dynasty was soon after replaced by Enlilite Gutians around 2450 B.C. But, when their reign in Mesopotamia was rejected, confusion swept over the region until an acceptable dynasty was established. The new dynasty came again from Lagash. Of the *patesi* in that line, the most influential include Urbau, who expanded the cultpower of the E.NINNU in Lagash as well as many other religious centers. Then, King Gudea cultivated even further abundance and economic prosperity by opening and securing trade routes.

With the death of Gudea's son, Ur-Dingirsu, no proper heir was brought forth and the dynastic line ended (c. 2250 B.C.) allowing the "seat of power" to be passed back to the old Sumerian city (and "Third Dynasty") of *Ur*, led by Ur-Engur (Ur-Nammu) who focused on the fortification of the Babylonian infrastructure, but with a reinstatement of the former "glory" of *Enlil* and the "Old Ways." His son, Dungi (better known as Shulgi), called himself the *High Priest* of *Anu* when he began to reinforce significance of the *Eridu* site and the legacy of *Enki*. But there is much more to this part of the story.

The patron deity of the famous Sumerian city, *Ur*, was the *Anunnaki god Nanna* (called "*Sin*" by the Babylonians, meaning "moon" and not literally "sin"). A long-standing Enlilite patronage to *Nanna-Sin* in *Ur* was maintained as payment for a "life-debt owed," when the *god* personally arranged the marriage between Ur-Nammu and "a high priestess of the Temple of Ur." In the balance of this, the dynasty of Ur sought a truly 'Sumerian' Renaissance, which fought hard to thwart any advancement of the Mardukites. [This prestigious city is remembered in biblical accounts as "*Ur of the Chaldeans*."]

Shulgi (also listed as Dungi) continued efforts toward an anti-Mardukite "Sumerian Renaissance" ushered in by his father's pact with *Nanna-Sin*. Economic and agricultural abundance was found under his reign, but uprisings and social rebellions sparked by this "new" Mardukite movement grew rather than diminished.

Further, Shulgi became a "lover" to the Enlilite *Anunnaki goddess queen Inanna-Ishtar*, and under her blessing began fighting newly formed "Nabu-tribes" (ancient Mardukites) in 2095 B.C. This continuing even after the mathematical shift to the Age of Aries—a task he passed down to his son, Amar-Sin (*A.Mar-Su.en*—"Son of the Moon God"), a tyrant king who unleashed vengeance on all (Mardukite) "rebels." The "Great War" ensued between 2048 and 2024 B.C., resulted, by some interpretations and records, in unleashing nuclear weapons (born of *alien* knowledge) against these pro-Mardukite westerners, the *Amorites*.

Akkadians knew of this group evolving on the outskirts of their Semitic lineage—the *Amurru* (Sumerian – *A.Mar-Tu*). This unique culture and language developed independent of the Sumerians, centralized around the cult-city center of Mari, west of the Euphrates, often referred to in lore as the "*Land of Martu*" (*Amar* to the Egyptians). Much like other Mardukite efforts in Enlilite territory, the Judeo-Christian biblical accounts reflect a harsh bias towards this culture of "Canaanites" stating in the *Book of Jubilees* (called the *Leptogenesis*) that: "The former giants, the *Rephaim*, gave way to the *Amorites*, an evil and sinful people whose wickedness surpasses that of any other, and whose life will be cut short on the earth."

Development of early Amorite ("Mardukite") culture contributed not only to the collapse of the *Ur III* Dynasty, but also to the founding of *Babylon* as a proper city-state and the division of Sumerian Mesopotamia into republic-styled Amorite Kingdoms, a system that remained primarily in effect for at least four centuries, from 2100 B.C. to 1700 B.C.

Amorite tribes first began forming in Mari (Syria) and Canaan around 2400 B.C. In biblical literature, "Amorite" and "Canaanite" appear synonymous. Three hundred years later (c. 2112 B.C.) the Amorites arrived onto the Mesopotamian scene during the confusion and chaos following the fall of the Akkadian Empire.

Nomadic Amorite hunter-gatherers, once preferring temporary shanty towns and tents over Enlilite Sumerian city life, began to adopt agriculture, homesteading and assimilated native Mesopotamian cultural systems as they re-stabilized the post-Sumerian world of *Babylonia*. Various kingdoms were established throughout the lands. Multiple city-states observed their own Amorite Dynasties, but only one would be responsible for launching a true Mardukite Empire—Hammurabi, famous King of Babylon.

— 4 —
BY THE CODE OF HAMMURABI
Building a Better Babylon and Beyond

"Whereas Sargon seems to have relied upon his power and his terror tactics to keep people under control, Hammurabi presents himself almost like a modern politician in that he wants to be loved; he wants the people to like him; he's going to set up laws that will protect them, not laws that will terrify them or force them into submission."

~ Amanda Podany, *California Polytech, Pomona*

In the post-Sumerian "Mardukite" era of Mesopotamia, Anunnaki traditions and systems were sealed under *Marduk*, heir-son of *Enki*. During this shift to the Age of Aries—the sign of *Marduk*, represented by the Ram—"divine politics" fueled religion, spirituality and the global reality experience.

The famous "creation stories" and "esoteric symbolism," serving as basis for all future traditions and societal reality systems, were forged onto cuneiform tablets of quasi-propaganda supporting a 'Babylonian' paradigm by the priest-scribes of ('led by' or 'dedicated to') *Nabu*, heir of *Marduk*.

A "Younger Generation" of Anunnaki become figures central to the structure of Mardukite Babylonian systems. These traditions are a direct evolution of the previous Sumerian legacy. It charts progression of a particular Anunnaki "family" in Mesopotamia and is not an arbitrary assimilation or recreation, as evident in similarly derived "Celestial" pantheons found elsewhere in "classical mythology."

Long after the vision put forth by Sargon, the next most famous and influential contributor to the legacy of a "Mardukite Babylon" was Babylonian King Hammurabi (1790 B.C. by the short chronology). In homage of *Marduk's* own legacy put forth in the *Enuma Eliš*—or *"Epic of Creation"*—King Hammurabi reconstructed the *ziggurat* temple-shrine and earth-home of the Anunnaki god *Marduk*, the E.SAG-ILA. The structure was once built in even more remote times in an attempt to establish a Mardukite "World Order" prematurely during Mesopotamia's early evolution – an effort brought down by the Enlilite Sumerians in the archetypal fall of the "Tower of Babel."

The region around *Babylon* hosted human occupation since at least the Third Millennium B.C. (the period of Sargon of Akkad around 2300 B.C.). That being said, the independent *Babylonian* city-state of the "Mardukite" legacy we know today was invigorated primarily by efforts from the Amorite Dynasty; specifically Hammurabi, who goes on to replace the former Enlilite Sumerian tradition in total with a complete Mardukite Babylonian establishment.

Under the reign of Hammurabi, Sumerian language became denationalized and scribes began recording all literature in the "new" Akkadian (Old Babylonian) language. This literary tradition accounts many pre-Assyrian era tablets of Babylonia found and translated today. This Babylonian literary revolution allowed a means to evolve a firmly rooted Anunnaki tradition with an emphasis on *Marduk* as the supreme "King of the Gods"—thus completely replacing the previously accepted Sumerian paradigm.

King Hammurabi is considered the greatest empire engineer since Sargon of Akkad, and in many ways was culturally and spiritually superior. Efforts conducted during his forty-two year reign allowed a centralized 'world government' of *Babylon* to form that not only served the people on an emotional, cultural and religio-spiritual level, but also reaching record-breaking energetic and monetary heights in global wealth, power and influence.

Ruling in honor of *Marduk* allowed Hammurabi to bring *Babylon* to fruition with cultural and spiritual heights that would not be visited again for at least a millennium—the Neo-Babylonian era of Nebuchadnezzar II.

Of the many conventions and systems first introduced to human civilization from *Babylon*, Hammurabi's legal code is one of the most significant to note—made popular in mass-consciousness as the "*eye for an eye*" methodology, but best known simply as the "Code of Hammurabi." While tyrannical and draconian penalties are the most frequently cited examples of the "Code," details of the 282 laws established, for the first time, a complete methodology of citizen rights, property rights, social rights and even feminine equality rights in addition to the creation of a "class" system.

The famous "Code of Hammurabi," by its own account, does not actually originate from Hammurabi's own thoughts. He considered himself merely a catalyst for the reign and power of something *greater* than himself—that of the patron deity, *Marduk*. The moral "Code" or Law of

Hammurabi, is what modern Mardukites call the *"Book of the Law of Marduk."* In the original Mardukite source book—*"The Complete Anunnaki Bible"** —*The Book of the Law of Marduk* is given as *Tablet-L* as it was given to the race of Dragonblood Kings—those who ruled in the name of Marduk on Earth.

Priests and priest-kings of *Babylon* ruled by a covenant: the descent of kingship on Earth from Heaven in honor of *Marduk* who granted freedom for men to rule in Mesopotamia as in Egypt. They did so in his name. And often took on his name and the name of his family members during their reign. But, after Hammurabi's death, an invasion by the Hittites broke this Babylonian dynasty, followed by a series of mysterious "sea-kings" that eventually spawn a second Babylonian dynasty and rise of the *Kassites*.

---

* Also available as *"Necronomicon: The Anunnaki Bible."*

— 5 —
THE KASSITE DYNASTY
Preserving the Legacies of Legends

When the *Old Babylonian* age ended, loose social organization and a broken political system left the empire open for a new dynastic power change. Fortunately for *Babylon*, a *pro-Marduk* force known as the Kassites came down (c. 1750 B.C.) from the Zagros Mountain region northeast of *Mesopotamia/Babylonia*. Kassite culture assimilated *Marduk* with their own deity-name, *Shuqamuna* (possibly from *Shakyamuni*, meaning "Buddha"). They defended *Mardukite Babylon* against years of struggle with the Hittites who sought to claim *Babylonia* for themselves.

In 1595 B.C. (some sources suggest 1651 B.C. depending on chronology), the Hittites successfully enter Babylon and "steal" *Marduk*. Historians usually interpret this to mean that they "*removed the image of Marduk*" from the temple— the main statue or *idol* representing the 'seat of power' in Babylon. Others might conclude that the Anunnaki god himself was actually captured while still residing on earth. In either case, the Kassites devoted over two decades in battle toward recovering and returning the "*idol*" to the temple. Overcoming tremendous struggles against the Hittites, by the grace of *Marduk*, the Kassite Dynasty established its own reign of *Babylon*, with few minor exceptions, for nearly half a millennium.

Kassites were a diplomatic people, enjoying trade relations with most of the known world, including Egypt, which was undergoing a spiritual revolution under the rule of Amonhotep IV (1350 B.C.), better known as Akhenaton. This new pharaoh changed the face of Egypt by installing his own "Mardukite" *Marduk-Aten- Ra Star-Religion*. Records survive to demonstrate that significant diplomatic correspondence exchanged between Akhenaton and at least two Kassite Kings: Kadashman Kharloe I and Burnaburiash II. These clay tablets are referred to by scholars as the "Amarna Letters"—all of which are written in *cuneiform* and not *Egyptian* characters. Scholars named the collection for the site where they were discovered at in 1887—*Tell el Amarna*—a modern Arabic name for of the ancient city of *Akhenaton*. Cuneiform tablet versions of Mesopotamian epics were also unearthed from there, most likely kept by Egyptian scribes and magician-priests for academic purposes.

Toward the end of their rule, the Kassites primary issues were no longer with the Hittites, but instead with a new rising force from the east, *Elam*. These Elamites replaced Mesopotamian dynasties with their own and also succeed in stealing a relic from *Babylon* to their city of *Susa*—the *stele* of the *Code of Khammurabi*. Sovereignty in *Mardukite Babylonia* begins to pass to those *most able*. Salvation of the land often required the "Eye and Hand of Marduk" to pass to foreigners as stewards in wait of launching a *Neo-Babylonian* empire— the "Fourth Dynasty of Babylon."

An *Assyrian* dynastic *patesi*, Marduk-Shapik-Zeri laucnhed campaigns to reunite the lands in 1200 B.C. This new northern "Assyrian" dynasty included Nabuchadnezzar I ("Nabu-kudur-ri-usur" in Assyrian, not to be confused with a later successor by the same name) who recovered the *stele* from the Elamites in 1125 B.C. But, real efforts toward a *Neo-Babylonian* empire were quickly thwarted by the Arameans and several small short-lived dynasties.

A true "*Babylonian Renaissance*" would have to wait for the proper visionary to manifest.

— 6 —
RISE OF THE ASSYRIANS
From Ashurbanipal to Nebuchadnezzar II

*"Even though the Assyrians were 'all powerful'
they still had their sense of cultural inferiority
—They saw Babylonia as the Source: the best
tablets; the 'real' cuneiform culture, much as in
the way 19th century Americans might have
looked to England as the place where you
would find 'real' English literature and such."*

~ Jerrold Cooper, *John Hopkins University*

Most historians consider *Assyrians* as simply an
extension of ancient Enlilite Sumerians, but
they are actually quite more than this. Most of
their history and lore, as with the rest of Mesopotamia, has been academically misappropri-
ated. Where the Kassites assisted in carrying
over "Mardukite" culture to post-Akkadian
Babylonia, the Assyrians were also custodians
of the legacy until the greatest heights of "Neo-
Babylonian Renaissance," witnessed under the
rule of Nebuchadnezzar II, the Chaldeo-Assyri-
an King of Babylon.

The "Assyrian" culture was named for a particular deity—*Assur* or *Ashur*. This name applied

to the people, the culture and the language, in addition to their native region of the name of their capital city. *Assur, Ashur, Assur, Asar, &tc.* —all of these are derived from an epithet for *Marduk*, the god of *Babylon*, and the Assyrians recognized this.

Academic "Assyriologists" ("Sumeriologists," *&tc.*) have often mistakenly attributed the chief Assyrian *Anunnaki god Ashur* ("*The One Who Sees*") with the chief deity observed in the original Sumerian pantheon: *Enlil*, or at the very least, his heir-son, *Ninurta-Ninib*. Mardukite records and deductive reasoning rooted in historical consistency would suggest this is not the case. Like true Babylonians, the Assyrians observed an Anunnaki tradition centered on *Marduk*, but of course in their own language.

The homeland of the *Assyrians*—their kingdom and realm—is more accurately an extension of the *Akkadian* culture—the "Old Babylonians." By 1000 B.C. the *Assyrians* had *Akkadians* populations of *Akkad* and became the next race of ancient-originating Semitic people in Mesopotamia. As with the Akkadians and Kassites once blessed by *Marduk* in times of need, arrival of *Assyrians* in *Babylon* eventually proved positive for its continuing legacy.

A Mardukite emphasis first returns to *Babylonia* with the reign of Nabu-mukin-apli (1000 B.C.) and the eighth dynasty of *Babylon*. This dynasty makes significant cultural efforts toward restoration of Mardukite temples and national statuary —all refinished in gold and *lapis lazuli*, the official "sacred" blue-hued stone of *Babylonia*. This period of peace, prosperity and cultural development began leading the population toward a true *Neo-Babylonian Renaissance*. But not everything was peaceful in Mesopotamia.

Babylonians experienced frequent uprising from western Sutu or Suti tribes: nomadic Enlilite Aramaean desert dwellers. Suti even prevented national religio-political festival ceremonies from occurring—on several occasions barring ceremonial procession of the Nabu statue from *Borsippa* (a site near *Babylon* sacred to the Babylonian scribe god) during the annual New Year Spring Equinox (*Akitu*, A.KI.TI or ZA-G.MUK) ceremony. [This national observance involving statuary idols was a symbolic reenactment of activities once observed of the Anunnaki themselves when they identifiably walked among the people of earth.]

During this struggle, Nabu-apla-iddina (while in *Babylon*) worked to maintain the highest peace with his rivals as possible, including the Assyrian king, Ashurnasipal II. He even formed a peace treaty with Ashurnasipal's son, King Shalmanesar II. Nabu-appla-iddina also launched a "literary" *Renaissance* in *Babylon* (and *Borsippa*), reviving the "Order of Nabu"—priest-scribes and magicians dedicated to salvaging and recopying older cuneiform tablets of esoteric, spiritual (religious), political, astronomical or scientific value. But, where *Sumerian* tablet-cycles were focused on antiquated establishments of world order, pantheistic hierarchies, divine politics and religion—we see something quite different in post-Sumerian paradigms of the *Assyrians*.

The Assyrian paradigm, foregoing religious and spiritual standards, emphasized battle, warfare and militant conquest, particularly what could be credited to a "Legacy of Kings." Where the previous Mesopotamian Kings were often respected for their role in establishing order by their working *with* the "gods" directly, the Assyrians spend their developmental years focused on territorial disputes and material conquests.

To their credit, however, the Assyrian Empire revolved around the most formidable military force known to the ancient world, introducing standards for many military innovations: cavalry, archery, siege engines, war ships, chariots, and battering rams.

Starting in the Ninth Dynasty of Babylon, King Nabu-nasir (750 B.C.) installed the "*Babylonian Chronicle*," a new practice of event recording for scribe-priests using a new local standard annual dating system—"A.N." (*Anno Nabonassan*). Other Kings in the dynasty included Nabu-nadin-zeri (735 B.C.), killed during a riot; and Nabu-suma-ukin II (732 B.C.), replaced after only one month by an Aramaen chief, Nabu-mukin-zeri. He was killed in a siege on *Babylon* by the Assyrians King Tiglath-Pileser III, founder of the Tenth Dynasty of Babylon and the "*Neo-Assyrian Empire*."

In 720 B.C., the throne was assumed by a Chaldean prince, Marduk-apla-iddina II (the biblical *Merodach-Baladan*). He struggled for control of *Babylon* against Sargon II, who succeeded in keeping him out of *Babylon* for over a decade. But after Sargon's death, Marduk-apla-iddina II resumed power of the throne and succeeded in sparking chaotic revolution in *Babylonia* before dying in exile (700 B.C.)—forcing Mesopotamia once again into political confusion for a time.

* * *

Eleven miles southwest of Babylon city, and many years before its modern rediscovery, archaeologist Henry Rawlinson began excavation (in the 1850's) of ruins of a different ancient city —*Borsippa*—sacred precinct of *Nabu*, Babylonian god of writing, cuneiform tablets and magic.

At first, archaeologists thought they had discovered the ruins of Babylon, but had found something else altogether—*Bad-Tibira* in the original Sumerian; or in Babylonian-Akkadian, the name reads *Til-Barsip*. Its present-day Arabic name is *Birs Nimrud*. Among these ancient remains—the E.ZIDA—*Nabu's* ziggurat, or else "*Temple of the Seven Spheres*," built on antiquated remains by the first major public Mardukite King—*Hammurabi*—and later restored by the last major Mardukite King—*Nebuchadnezzar II*. [It is from this temple and others in Babylon that the "Seven-fold Order" significant to the "Mardukite Babylonian Anunnaki Tradition" are derived.]

An avid reader and collector of all tablets available in Mesopotamia, the "Royal Library" archives of the Assyrian King, *Ashurbanipal*, maintained a complete record of everything that could be recorded—but in the Assyrian language. This so vastly influenced early archaeologists that scholars named the entire academic field after the collection—"Assyriology." Such intellectual pursuits, however, were not always so prominent among leadership in Mesopotamia as many of the rulers spent most of their time and energies maintaining or expanding their physical realm through battle and conquest.

Coinciding with the death of *Ashurbanipal* came the fall of Assyrian power in Babylon. The Babylonians elected a king from among their own revolutions—*Nabopolassar*. He then joined forces with the *Chaldeans* and the *Medes* in defeating the Assyrians at their capital of *Nineveh*, and then later the *Egyptians*. Aging and war-worn after several successful victories against two empires, he wisely passed power of the throne and the realm to his son, while still alive. His son—the famous Mardukite King, *Nebuchadnezzar II*.

King Nebuchadnezzar II supported a prosperous pro-*Mardukite* era for nearly fifty years. He maintained peaceful unity of *Sumer* and *Akkad* (*Babylonia*) in the name of *Marduk* and *Nabu*. He restored many city centers and sacred ziggurat temples. Before his death, he predicted an impending end to the glory of his *Chaldean Empire in Babylon*—and the actions of the kings who were to be his successors invariably proved him right. [See also the *Mardukite Tablet-S Series*.]

The city of Babylon served as a geographic capital of the entire "*Babylonian Empire*." As a dynamic city-state, the conditions of Babylon constantly adjusted to change in accordance with the forces in play, but one ideal remained constant: the relentless determination to reach an apex of esteem and glory—and according to their tradition, reign by *Divine Right*.

Installation of "*Mardukite World Order*" into human consciousness continued to radiate from the city of Babylon; its *Mardukite* designation being, literally—"*Babylon*"—from the Akkadian *bab.ilu*, meaning "*Gateway of the Gods*" or "*Star-Gate to Heaven*." [In Sumerian, the name is written as the logograms: "KA.DINGIR.RA. KI."]

Walking in the shadows of a legacy born from ancient icons—*Sargon* and *Khammurabi*—the third and last legendary "Mardukite King" brought Babylon to unforeseen heights during reign of the *Neo-Babylonian (Chaldean) Dynasty*—*Nebuchadnezzar II*. Following the years of chaotic discord in *Babylonia* and irreverence in the *holy city*, all that had been built or could be restored proper to the national gods—*Mard-*

uk and *Nabu—Nebuchadnezzar II* commissioned in Babylon during his lifetime.

Before Nabuchadnezzar's death, his heir-son, Awel-Marduk (560 B.C.), also written Amel-Marduk ("Evil Marduk"), reigned for only two years. He usurped the throne against his father's will (who was still in power) and was murdered by his brother-in-law and successor Nergal-sharezer, in assistance to true kingship. None again would be as great as Nabuchadnezzar II. Any short-lived reform efforts to maintain integrity of *Babylonia* were therefore quickly dissolved by one of the most unjust anti-Mardukite Kings of *Babylon* (555 B.C.) in the midst of an otherwise perfect *Mardukite Renaissance*.

Following the death of Nabuchadnezzar II and its chaos, the "Seat of Babylon" was usurped by an Assyrian rebel calling himself *Nabonidus*. His name meant "*Nabu is exalted*," though his suppression of the Mardukites, desecration of holy sites and violation of countless traditions would indicate that he lived by another creed. *Nabonidus* fell prey to the old Sumerian "cult of the moon god"—the lunar-cult associated with the Anunnaki god *Nanna-Sin*. *Nabunidus* chose the pre-Babylonian Enlilite "lunar cult" in lieu of following the solar (and stellar traditions) of the Mardukite Babylonians. He even forbid the

Mardukite *Akiti* (*Akitu*) "New Year" festival of the spring equinox from taking place. Marduk was forced to take action, whether literally or in spirit. To prevent the utter annihilation of his people, the "Eye and Hand of Marduk" would again fall upon foreigners.

Cyrus the Great marched on Babylon and dethroned Nabonidus, igniting the Persian Dynasty of Babylon. His first action upon entering the city—to pray, make sacrifice and participate in nationalist ceremonies at the "Temple of Marduk." In fact, he attributed all of his success in taking control of *Babylon* to the power of the *Anunnaki god* Marduk. [This is recorded on the *Mardukite Tablet-L Series*.] His lineage is allowed to continue until the arrival of, and replacement by, the Greek Hellenistic Dynasty of Alexander the Great in 330 B.C.

And the rest, as they say: *Is history...*

— 7 —
CUNEIFORM TABLETS AND THE ORIGINS OF WRITING
The Birth of World Systematization

"The education of the Babylonians was entirely in the hands of the priests, who derived their knowledge from Nabu, the inventor of writing and letters, and every kind of learning — the Lord of "Houses of Tablets" (or books), i.e. the first libraries."

~ E.A. Wallis Budge, *Babylonian Life & History*

The overt observable evolution of Sumerian civilization into a *Babylonian Empire*—the facts —as described previously regarding history, may not altogether seem remarkable on the surface. However, the *seeker* should keep in perspective just how quickly all of this developed from seemingly nothing. It is true that societal living was originally organized around *state religion*, but prior to this it was culminated not by social relationships shared between people, but by their living relationship with the earth. Where first we have loosely organized nomadic hunter-gatherers forced to wander about or dwell in caves, essentially rolling the dice of chance for their survival, very little time passes before sweeping urbanization of Mesopotamia, developed around structured agricultural farming and pasturing.

Mesopotamia may be credited with many "*firsts*" during the development of early human history. It is, however, the incorporation and evolution of "writing" that the Sumerians are most esteemed for—something undoubtedly developed by necessity for continuous civic growth, spiritual and scientific progression. In fact, it is *only* with *writing* that we have *any* concept at all of "history." Everything *prior* to this inception for our times, is rightfully considered "prehistoric"—those times accompanied by no written records.

According to ancient cuneiform tablets, the original decision to cultivate civilization in Mesopotamia was not born from men, but from distinct beings known as the *Anunnaki*—those appearing to "come down from the sky"; later treated as *deities* and *gods* of the original "divine pantheon"—those who "decree the fate on Earth." Cuneiform tablets describe Anunnaki motives for "genetically upgrading" humanoids: to make them fit as material workers for these "*gods*."[*] This started long before what we call the "*Deluge*," under the direction of these "divine" *overseers*—not yet the mortal priest-kings found in popular historical chronicles—prior to what we know as "*human* civilization."

Anunnaki control of the "heavens" and "aerospace" rested with the god Anu and his son Enlil, respectively. The material world, however—the realm most integrated with human life—became the domain of Anu's other son, E.A., called *Enki* in Babylon—whose name means "Lord (*En*) of the Earth (*Ki*)" in Babylon. While the majority of ancient Mesopotamia was classified "Enlilite" territory, origins for the esoteric "Arts of Civilization" emerge from *Enki's* own southern city of *Eridu* on the ancient coasts of the Persian Gulf. Here we find systematic origins of "true" human civilization. Born of innate necessity and survival of material systems, use of esoteric "*Secret Doctrines*" allowed data to condition the human psyche through integration of "worldly systems." The means by which this has always been executed on earth: "*media*"—the *written word*.

---

[*] *Tablet-G* in "*The Complete Anunnaki Bible*" and "*Anunnaki Bible: Cuneiform Scriptures (New Standard Zuist Edition)*."

It is evident that practically all ancient cultural "mythologies" share a unique anthropological belief: that indigenous humans were somehow "engineered" apart from their natural evolving timeline on the planet, and further given a knowledge of something "outside of themselves" that was directly responsible for this. *Cuneiform tablets* speak of this "outside" and "intervening" force as a group of beings called *Anunnaki*—though they are known by a myriad of other names as well, particularly among diverse cultures and languages around the globe.

According to the *cuneiform* texts, the *Anunnaki* sought to prepare the earth for habitation, but found the physical nature of the work on earth was not suited to them. They employed their "army"—known as the IGIGI ("Watchers")—to do manual labor. And after some years pass, even this group revolts. The *Anunnaki* hesitantly decide to upgrade existing hominids, fashioning a new class of "worker."

Today, we now see a cliché concept emerging in the "New Age" that acknowledges humans as a slave-species built by and for "gods"—or at least these "Anunnaki" figureheads later interpreted as the mythological "gods" of antiquity. The *Sumerians* and *Babylonians* weren't "stupid." The "mythologies" reflected in their writ-

ing are not drawn from ignorance or people unaware of "natural phenomenon." Skeptical
scholars minimize the true significance of history by putting forth fallacies. Cuneiform literature left behind suggests a highly intellectual
and spiritual culture with a deep understanding
of the *cosmos* from the beginning, even when
expressed though a limited vocabulary.

Much like early Egyptians using hieroglyphics,
the first Sumerian "cuneiform" writing (named
in Classical times from the Latin "*cuneus*,"
meaning "wedge") was also a tradition of picture-writing etched with sticks and fingernails.
Refinement of the writing style continued
throughout the *Sumerian* age, but around 2100
B.C., the script-form changed dramatically with
a gift from *Nabu* for his Babylonian scribe-
priests—the reed *stylus* pen. There are many
who seem easily dismissive of the current subject matter in this book, or that simply find the
topic of *cuneiform tablets* to be boring and
without relevance. As a monumental cornerstone in human development, the perfection of
writing in Babylon is the very reason we have
such vast collections available today to glean
lore of this extraordinary and forgotten empire.
Without this specific esoteric literary tradition,
we would be left clueless.

* * *

Early picture-writing proved sufficient for many things. The goals of its use were simple—primarily survival. Hunting grounds, natural dangers and even some elaborate stories could all be marked with a primitive pictorial language. Humans navigated obstacles of communication easily enough using speech and gesture—so, what then was the purpose of writing?—of the *words that stay?*

All of the civic systems on the planet, those that distinguish the "elevated" social network of the "human animal," depend on a communication relay of the written word to be effective. And with creation of the stylus, this was accessibly possible—a methodology for "systems" was broadcast wide among the masses. Its successful implementation aided Anunnaki "control" of an exponentially growing human population. But it was a "Mardukite" inception—the result of two efforts: the birth of systems in *Eridu* by *Enki* (with the aid of, not surprisingly, his heir-son Marduk), and also the ratification of writing in *Babylon* by *Nabu* (heir-son of Marduk) much later. By combining these two facets, the "Arts of Civilization" were activated in Babylonia.

The human psyche became conditioned to societal living, now connecting two aspects internally: *pictures* and *words*. The two were already one in form—as picture writing—but only in the vaguest sense. Use of a *stylus* changed this by not only speeding up the flow and form of written images, but as a straight-edged tool, this pen eliminated *curvature* of any characters. No longer would someone have need to draw out an image of several animals to depict them. A series of quick hashed-wedge marks could represent it instead; and for standard-issue human consciousness, the two would become associatively inseparable in meaning.

Solidification of abstract concepts and ideas represented as "words" actually changes how the brain thinks—changes the way in which one experiences these aspects of reality and what the words actually represent. Mentally adopting a label system for fixed nouns and names creates an internal database called a 'schema' which manipulates experiences and affects memory. An academic consensus is that these "perceptions" are evolutionary advantages, adapting one to the environment that an individual is reared to. This certainly was not evolutionarily necessary for the survival of the species, but for the survival of the *system*, by which matters of commerce and state, laws and government, roles and order, religion and trade could all be *fixed* to writing, securing an imprinted history and fate on the human consciousness to *words that stay*.

The cuneiform wedge-writing system is designed quite differently than more recently used classical alphabets, such as the "Roman" letters this book is printed in. In fact, cuneiform is not an alphabet at all, but a series of symbols used to represent phonetic sounds or "syllables"—typically combinations of a consonant and a vowel. Thus, we have no ancient cuneiform form of a letter "*B*," but there are signs for the sounds: *ab*, *ib*, *ub*, *ba*, *be*, *bi* and *bu*.

Babylonian refined *stylus*-based cuneiform, combined with the ease of clay tablet construction, resulted in a plethora of written records in the ancient world. Eventually, a "royal library" was established in *Babylonia* (often in *Borsippa*) as a Temple of Nabu, maintained by the official librarian-priest sometimes known as a *Rab Girginakki* in Akkadian language. Efforts to create and preserve similar "archival libraries" later occurred throughout Mesopotamia—always under the direction of the current *authority* in power. By 2000 B.C., Babylonian law required all transactions be documented and duplicated by official *scribe-priests*.

While writing itself was prevalent, for an exceptionally long period of human history, only higher classes of citizen were required to learn reading and writing. Dependency on scribe-priests as "interpreters of writing" among the common masses became great. Any indiscretion or falsehoods relayed in this process were severely punished, which strengthened the faith of the people in these "life-depending" (and "life defining") public records and deeds of ownership.

By necessity, the *cylinder-seal* was developed—a clay signature-seal uniquely fashioned for an individual and often worn or carried like a large bead long before signet rings. This small cylinder could be *rolled* across a tablet surface to create a rectangular stamp-mark. And just to be sure there was no tampering, the Nabu scribe-priests developed a unique way of enclosing and preserving signed clay tablets within clay envelopes with a duplicate signed inscription on the outside. In special circumstances an additional copy would be retained by the archivist. These practices promoted the original form of banking and commerce—trading in kind, complete with a notarized receipt. If this were not enough, a new *system* of conceptual civic wealth was integrated: the possession of land property—or *real estate*—authorized and governed by the state, ownership of which was not represented by physical occupancy, but by *written deeds*.

The full implications of these *Anunnaki*, *Babylonian*, and "*Mardukite*" systems are not so obvious to the common man—and certainly not to early "Assyriologists" either. Seldom do we consider the covert governing body that originally dictated these systems and regulated their integration into social consciousness. Such might be easily overlooked or taken for granted by contemporary minds thinking of little than one-foot-in-front-of-the-other. And yet it is entirely connected to where humans are, were and will be.

Definitions, semantics, knowledge boundaries and the ability to coherently and permanently record them into histories, calendars, maps, property deeds and even "secret esoteric knowledge"— completely and utterly changed the reality experience for the Human Condition... *forever!*

— 8 —

THE PRIEST-SCRIBES OF NABU
The Secret Society of Mardukite Babylon

"The Palace of Ashurbanipal, King of the World, King of Assyria, who in Assur and Belit puts his trust, on whom Nabu and Tasmitu have bestowed broad ears, who has acquired clear eyes. The valued products of the scribe's art, such as no one among the kings who has gone before me had acquired, the wisdom of Nabu, unequaled, as so much as can be found, I have had inscribed on tablets and arranged in groups. I have revised, and for the sign of my reading, have set in my Palace this library— I, the ruler, who knows the Light of Assur, the King of the Gods."

~ King Ashurbanipal, *Royal Library Dedication*

What academic scholars term *"Babylonian Mythology"* is actually an evolution of the former *Sumerian Anunnaki* legacy—the progression of an archetypal *Anunnaki* family in Mesopotamia and *not* simply a fanciful cultural assimilation or reapplication of a similar pantheon. This is what we see in later classical *mythoi*, such as the Greeks and Romans, which simply regurgitate the same ancient themes with new names.

In similar fashion, the esoteric (religious) Mardukite Babylonian political pantheon is as an extension of the older former Sumerian one. This gives rise to misunderstandings, prompting misconceptions and misinterpretation of tablets from varying origins and time periods. In this case, however, Mardukite Babylonian spiritual, religious, cultural and political focus is transferred to activities of a "younger generation" of *Anunnaki gods*; coherently "sealed" in the Star-Gate System of Babylonian Mystical Tradition.

In the "Mardukite" Babylonian paradigm, Anu's position as "heavenly father" (turned "grandfather" by the "younger generation") remains unchallenged, and retains the numeric designation of 60, the perfect *whole* number (like our 100) in Mesopotamian mathematics. Controlling more worldly concerns—the position of "earthly father" for the local universe (numerically designated the rank of 50), is a title first bestowed to *Enlil*, royal heir of *Anu* according to "Enlilite" Sumerian tradition. *Enlil's* heir-son— *Ninurta* or *Ninib*—was next in succession to continue the "Enlilite" legacy. Although *Enki* was given the role of "Lord of the Earth" (with a numeric designation of 40), the division between the domains of *Enlil* and *Enki* blur—both literally and figuratively.*

In the Sumerian paradigm *Enlil* and *Enki* aid one another in the foundation of the material world, but by the time of the Babylonians, each had their own dedicated following—essentially splitting the global population into dualism.

According to early Babylonian tablets, this schism first occurred concerning the genetic upgrade of original humans themselves, and then over their "disposal" during the *Deluge. Enlil,* an *Anunnaki* nationalist, high commander and heir to *Anu,* was understandably reserved about the creation and assistance of humans. *Enki,* the chief scientist and esoteric magician of the *Anunnaki* (with a dynastic line that is not granted the same royal distinction as *Enlil*), sees potential in the human race to preserve his own legacy on earth and that of his son, *Marduk.*

As cuneiform writing evolved, the face of the religion changed and crystallized into more familiar versions of the Mesopotamian mysteries it is defined by today. Mystical and religious

---

* Refer to "*Sumerian Religion*" or "*Anunnaki Gods*" by Joshua Free for additional details concerning individual Anunnaki deities.

tablets were avidly created in Babylon to not only solidify and protect the traditions, but actually *manipulate* them. This primitive logic is a basis for many semantic *systems* still active today. In short—reality is based on the experience of the *realm*, the world of light that we see and acknowledge stimuli from. The world of light is separated into *forms*, which require *classification* as "things." These *classifications* must work together within a coherent *system* to carry any conceptual or functional meaning. [This is what enables the current author to write these *words* and a reader to comprehend them *later*.]

While basis of writing is to collect "data," it is the interpretation within consciousness that equates it to *facts*. "*Words that stay*" are "*facts*" collected about *reality*—the internal processing of cohesive *experience*. In ancient Mesopotamia, we find historical tablets detailing deeds of kings and cosmological tablets describing the deeds of gods—these are the *beliefs* about *reality* dictated for the population and presented as *facts*.

Conclusively, as far as the human condition is concerned: the *written word dictates reality*. And to be fair, while men and kings go to their graves each believing in their own truth, these thousands of years later, it is the *written word* from their era that has survived them all.

* * *

Mardukite priests of Babylon were, by nature, *Priests of Enki*, following a tradition from the ancient *systems* born in *Eridu*. Beyond simply *collecting data* to support a public belief system, the first pragmatic mystical and religious use of writing was the recording of ("esoteric") *Secret Doctrines* and ("exoteric") *incantations* —used later religiously as *appeals* to the *gods* for material worldly assistance. This developed more *"figuratively"* over time as the temple-shrine *ziggurat*-homes of the *Anunnaki gods* themselves became occupied instead by worldly representatives of the same roles.

In the beginning, people were instructed to petition their needs to the temple-priests, who would in turn make appropriate offerings and incantations to the deity involved. This *system* is still installed in society today—in both religion and politics—where ministers or authorities act as intermediaries between citizens and perceptibly "higher powers." Here we see a distinction between the *exoteric* "surface world" *system*-religion of public opinion and participation, separate from *esoteric* practices and traditions of the scribe-priests, temple-priests and priest-kings themselves.

> The *scribes* research and write the tablets,
> the *temple-priests* enact the tablets, and
> then the *kings* enforce the tablets.

Mardukite Babylon could hardly be considered ruled by Marduk's own lineage—but all of *Babylonia* was still maintained under his care by way of "chosen" priest-kings who were nearly all under the influence of a prestigious secret society—one that changed the shape of Mesopotamia, and the remaining world there-after, with nearly two millennium of unbroken covert operation in *Babylonia*: the *Priest-Scribes of Nabu*.

An unusually enigmatic figure in Mesopotamian history, *Nabu* is listed only among the Babyloni-an "Mardukite" hierarchy of *Anunnaki gods*. His numeric designation is 12—indicative of cycles, time and esoteric knowledge or "magic." *Nabu* is heir-son to the dynasty of *Marduk*, born of *Sarpanit*, an earth-born wife taken by *Marduk*. She was technically "human," but descended directly from *Adapa*, the first genetically up-graded human by the *Anunnaki god Enki*, known in Egypt as "Ptah." This makes *Nabu* earth-born and little more than half-divine.

Nabu shared the dynasty of *Marduk* (whose faces are also the Egyptian *Ra*, *Amon* and *Aten*) with an estranged brother, named *Sutu* (also *Satu* or *Sati*, the Egyptian "*Seth*"), whose name means *mountain* or *life of the mountain*. Another "half-brother rival" is listed as *Asar* (the Egyptian "*Osiris*").

The name 'Nabu' ("*who speaks for*") indicates a "herald" or "announcer." The word also made its way into the Semitic-Hebrew language as *nabih*, meaning "prophet."

By the time of "Old" *Mardukite Babylon*—around 2150 B.C., corresponding with the "Age of Aries," the end of the *Old Kingdom* in Egypt and the launch of the "royal" *Dragon Court* by Ankhfn-khonsu—the temple-city and cult center of Nabu was localized near *Babylon* at *Borsippa*.

In Babylon, earthborn *Nabu* is transferred the epithet "*Tutu*"—replacing a previous Sumerian agricultural goddess, *Nisaba*, briefly given credit for pictorial *cuneiform* in Sumerian tradition. As *Nabu-Tutu* he reflects a "*druidic*" role—the Babylonian "nature-deity" called upon at the New Year Festival of *Akiti* to bless the crops and provide fertile land. By that same paradigm, *Marduk* would be a "sky-deity," representing a domain of the starry sun that shines down on the land.

In this ancient literary tradition, *Nabu* represents the epitome of the "*pen is mightier than the sword.*" Where previous *Anunnaki gods* had cultivated civilization with their contributions—the *cattle and grain* had already been brought, the *pickax* had already been given, *&tc.*—Nabu offers the *reed stylus* and reformation of cuneiform writing. This sparked renewed interest in the arts of *Eridu*—the *Secret Doctrines* of esoteric "magic" and science from *Enki* and *Marduk*.

Writing allowed the "*Arts of Civilization*" to be systematized on records of an *Ancient Mystery School*, and *Nabu* became a custodial guardian of these "Tablets of Destiny"—powerful "information" that "sealed" material creation (or cosmic ordering) to the *Divine Right* of the *Anunnaki*.

As the "Keeper of Secrets," *Nabu* proved necessary in developing the literary tradition that allowed *Babylon* and the supremacy of *Marduk* to be possible. *Nabu* was a mastermind in the company of the most intelligent beings in this corner of the Universe. In the establishment of *Babylon*, *Nabu* was successful in developing his own unique cult following that was often rivaling that of even *Marduk*.

The original "cult" of *Nabu* still exists even to this day as an underground esoteric sect called the "Mardukite Chamberlains."

The magic and mysticism of *Babylonia*—born in *Eridu*, then extrapolated and reformed by Mardukite Priest-Magicians and the *Order of Nabu*—was restricted to the priests and treated wholly religious in nature, but rooted in the ancient power and technologies of the *gods*. "Magical" texts from this age are primarily hymns and prayers. The later doctrines or scriptures made public, first originated as historical documents among Mesopotamians, cuneiform tablets chronicling creation and universal order, the genesis of man, the flood cycle and the eventual restoration of civilization. These were all later reinterpreted by other cultures as their own.

Responsibility for forging and preserving this Babylonian literary tradition on clay tablets rested with the *Order of Nabu*, a secret force that sought to shape the history and future legacy of Babylon in dedication to *Marduk*.

In view of the fact that mystical traditions of Enki remain popular beneath the surface of the occult today, there is widespread familiarity with the Typhonian archetype from Babylon of "*Marduk-versus-Tiamat*," interest is rising in the Babylonian systems and Anunnaki traditions and other derivatives of Freemasonry and Illuminati sects—it is the present author's opinion that the efforts of the ancient *Order of Nabu* proved successful in establishing a permanent Anunnaki Legacy for Mardukites of Babylon.

— 9 —
MARDUKITE MONOLATRY
The "Star Religion" of Babylon & Egypt

"Marduk's rise to supremacy did not end polytheism—the religious belief in many gods. On the contrary, his supremacy required continued polytheism, for to be supreme to other gods, the existence of other gods was necessary. He was satisfied to let them be, as long as their prerogatives were subject to his control; but what Marduk expected was that they come and stay with him in his envisaged Babylon— prisoners in golden cages, one may say."

~ Zecharia Sitchin, *Earth Chronicles: End of Days*

The Babylonian *"Star Religion"* of *Marduk* sought to "occult" and conceal the previously laden Sumerian religious designations of the *Elder Gods*. Early Sumerian traditions were not very systematic, or even a true "religion," making them easily overlapped by the first clearly defined *systemology*—one that served as an archetype for all later human civilization on the planet. Directly exported forms of this stellar cult included Hermetic Tradition, Atenism, Zoroastrianism, Mithraism, and of course the Semitic-Judeo system.

Original systems integrated into human consciousness were not at first the "monotheism" defined by academic scholars. This appeared later when *Enlilite* standards transformed into *Jehovah* or the Christian "God" as a single personification. In Hebrew, *El* (*Enlil*) and *Ia-Yah-weh* (*Enki*) are separate beings, a belief debated the early Christian Yahwist and Elohist sects.

Later Christian authorities likened the ancient myths to "One God" surrounded by *"lesser angels,"* but this still does not adequately explain the anthropomorphic manifestation of the One God on earth being the same as, one-to-one: The Absolute, The All-present, The All-knowing, The All-powerful "Divine Source." We see remnants of this distinction in Gnostic Mysticism, early Elohist Christianity and, of course, modern Mardukite and Mardukite Zuism interpretations.

Contemporary historians often simplify, likening the Mardukite stellar-cult to a religious "monotheistic" standard. But the tradition is more correctly termed: *monolatrism*. This is a confusing concept for some—probably remaining so as much today as in ancient times—as even the Assyrians were completely *pantheistic*, exalting *Assur* (*Marduk*), but venerating and working with many other "personal deities" as representations of the "Divine."

Babylon became the "seat of the gods," but by Mardukite standards, this was intended differently than either *monotheism* or *polytheism* can provide. The basic program became as follows: There are many *gods* but the way is through *One*, idealized in Babylonian tradition as *Marduk* and his consort *Sarpanit* via the holy receptionists, *Nabu* ("Divine Secretary" or "Librarian of Babylon") and his consort *Teshmet* (or *Tasmit*), the "Listener of Prayers."

The work performed to usurp the ancient *Fifty Names* from the *Enuma Eliš* ("*Epic of Creation*") for Marduk also illuminates the idea of "many *gods* as *One*" or the "*One* manifest with many *faces*," but with the central figure on earth always returning to Marduk as *divine representative*. Assuming the *Fifty Names* connected to an ancient "Divine Decree" of "Fifty" ("Ninnu")—by Anunnaki numeric designation of World Order, equaling the rank of *Enlil*, the "Lord of Command."

Babylonian myth and magic systems are dedicated to *Marduk's* "Divine World Order." It is illustrated through the original mystical "kabbalah" system: *ten gates*, *two doors* and *seven levels*—just like the design for *Marduk's ziggurat*—E.TEMEN.AN.KI—*"The Temple of Heaven and Earth."*

These *Ziggurats*—artificial "mountain-home temple-shrines of the gods"—stood as giant stepped-pyramids in honor of the patron deity of a city-state, so named from the *Akkadian* word for them: *"Zi-kur-ra-tu."* And each ancient Mesopotamian city had one. Of course, stepped pyramids are not only found in Mesopotamia—but many other prehistoric cultures, too. They are unique in function as "residences," seldom seen in more traditional Egyptian pyramids. However the oldest pyramids of Egypt are actually stepped-pyramids.

In Mesopotamia, extraordinarily large stepped pyramids elevated the temple buildings, shrines and astronomical observatories. Yet they were built and rebuilt on foundations for infrastructure that once served as the mundane earthly homes for a star-race of "gods"; as observed by the most ancient religious systematization on the planet.

```
EVOLUTION OF MAGICAL SYSTEMS

Sumerian:        Unity, celestial-cosmic
Babylonian:      Hierarchy, temple-reli-
                   gions
Egyptian/Hermetic:    Names, magical-
                        mysticism

Sumerian:        Petition to the Most High
Babylonian:      Petition to a pantheon
Egyptian/Hermetic:    Petition to hier-
                        archy of spirits
```

The "Systemology" of Mardukite Babylonian Religion reflects many aspects of *animism* and *pantheism*—the belief that everything possesses an innate or inherent "spirit" or *Divine Spark* that entangles it to the "eternity of the cosmos" or the *All-as-One* (*Divine Source*). This "everything" includes fragmentation of distinct personalities or "Self." Cuneiform tablets distinguish these aspects as *utukku* (the *Divine Spark* or animating "spiritual essence") and *edimmu* (the "identity program" or soul of the body). In the related Egyptian tradition, these aspects are equated to the *ka* (life-force) and *ba* (personality) of an individual being.

Nabu-scribes forged the *Enuma Eliš*—a kind of cosmogenetic "*Epic of Creation*" central to the religion. But, the political purpose of this document was to bestow Marduk with the "*Tablets of Destiny*," enabling him world control or World Order. The covert cosmological beliefs were, however, actually *monistic*. This means that the *Divine Source* represents a single unifying principle, agent or "element" (referred to in some materials as the *All-as-One*) defining:

One Existence — One Truth — One Cosmic Law.

The later philosophy and practices of *Hermetic mysticism* are, therefore, not "invented" during the classical age, but are actually imported from a more antiquated *Ancient Mystery School* born in Babylon.

— 10 —
MARDUK & THE ANUNNAKI
Mesopotamian Mythology of Babylon

"Like Napolean, who decided he did not need to be crowned according to the rules and crowned himself without further ado, so the Assyrian priests gave the honor to Ashur simply by taking the old Babylonian tablets and recopying them, substituting the name of their own god for that of Marduk. The work was not very carefully done, and in some places the name of Marduk still creeps in..."

~ Edward Chiera, *They Wrote on Clay*

In addition to implementing a social civic systematization, the Babylonian literary tradition focused primarily on one key element for associating its knowledge: *religious myths*. The Mesopotamian "mythos" is not called such to indicate it as *fictions*. The real meaning of a *mythos* or *mythoi* (plural) in human history concerns the *systemology* of human consciousness —a cultural paradigm of reality. It is taken out of context in contemporary understanding, often belittled as fanciful legends from confused primitives. It is perhaps only in the "New Age" niches of present time that we find a true and honest interest in these ancient cultures of yesterday and what they have to offer us for today, as we step forward into tomorrow.

In short: a "mythology" was once little more than cultural documentation of history, along with its varied narratives carried by word of mouth, accounting for the deeds of gods, demigods and kings. Cultural emphasis on specific characters and themes as represented in the societal knowledge, is what, in essence, *creates* a mythology—a way of seeing the world as shared by a large group. It didn't take long for this methodology to be *covertly manipulated* to serve the political integrity of the *Babylonian Empire*.

Historically, spiritual and religious "mythology" emphasizes a particular activity that few individualsrelate to today—human interaction with the "*gods*." Descriptions of these encounters commonly involve a particular geographic feature—*mountains*. And where mountains were not accessible, the *gods* worked in conjunction with *humans* to construct "artificially built mountains" or "*zikkurat*"-*pyramids*—(more commonly spelled "*ziggurat*" in English) but named from the Akkadian "*zaqaru.*" In older Sumerian languages, the word for mountain was also *kur*; same as the "primordial dragon" of the cosmos as it appears in pre-Babylonian mythology.

Surviving cuneiform tablet-sources intermittently make mention of "*dragons*." At some juncture; the "universe," the "planet earth" and the "blood of men" are all coined "dragon" in nature. The first legendary figures confronting "dragons" become *archetypes* for the "King of the Mountain."* In the most ancient Sumerian versions, these are Enlil, Ninurta and even Inanna-Ishtar. Given the "Enlilite" patina on this early cycle of records, the name of Marduk appears nowhere on original tablet epics of Sumer.

During the early Sumerian age, Marduk—called ASARLULI—was the first "magician-priest" of *Eridu*. This antediluvian cult center was later known in legend to the Greeks in their own language and mythic interpretation as the "*Temple of Poseidon*." Therefore, although there are many "lost civilizations" on the planet, scholars have confused semantics regarding the Greek renderings of "*Atlantis*"—information they recovered from the Egyptians long after the fact. At any rate, Marduk is primarily kept occupied in *Eridu* during the pre-Babylonian Sumerian era.

---

*   See also *"Draconomicon"* by Joshua Free.

The Mardukite Babylonian "*Epic of Creation*" (academically named "*Enuma Eliš*") was often observed and revered in ancient traditions for its *systemological* value, even above its "*cosmogenetic*" qualities. However, it is *set* in a time before "earth" or "men" and describes the evolution of them both out of an unfolding "created universe"—progressive "*fragmentation*" of the *All-as-One* into parts. This has esoteric implications quite unique to ancient "Mardukite" lore and modern Systemology. Already fragmented beings themselves, the "*Anunna-(ki)*" used the "Secret Doctrines of the Cosmos," to their advantage when systematically dealing with "humans"—and the programming of the Human Condition.*

In the "*Enuma Eliš*" we are given a political account of Marduk slaying the "cosmic serpent" or *dragon*, representing his "overcoming of chaos" in the cosmos to establish his own universal or "world order." This was actually an "old concept" revived from pre-Babylonian (Sumerian) use of the *kur* in earlier mythologies. By performing this feat or conquest, Marduk became the "*King of the Anunnaki*," a title was bestowed upon him (according to the "*Enuma Eliš*") as a reward from the "*Council of*

---

* See also "*The Tablets of Destiny*" by Joshua Free.

Anunnaki" for his dragon-slaying feat. Performing this feat, even if only symbolically and in archetypal consciousness, the "Mardukite" forces are given *Divine Right* to exercise the powers of the *Anunnaki* on Earth.

The *Enuma Eliš* forms the cornerstone of Mardukite usurpation of the Sumerian Anunnaki hierarchy. The work also illustrates a distinction between eras of older generations: a race of "*Ancient Ones*" led by the primordial dragon, TIAMAT; "Elder Gods" or *Anunna* of prehistorical renown, such as *Anu*, *Enlil* and *Enki*; and a "Younger Generation" of *Anunnaki* in the Babylonian pantheon under *Marduk,* which included many of his Enlilite peers: *Nanna-Sin, Inanna-Ishtar, Samas (Shammash)* and *Nergal*.

While in *Eridu*, *Marduk* is not actually attributed among early Sumerian *Anunnaki* gods— not listed among the pantheon. In fact, *Marduk* is initially the primary high-ranked leader of the IGIGI ("Watchers") and during this role sets a new *status quo* in *Eridu*—and then in *Babylon* —concerning intermarriage between *Anunnaki* with humans, as described on ancient cuneiform tablets. For this "indiscretion," by Enlilite "World Order" standards, he was denied any future *Divine Right*. His argument remained that he was never going to be given his "*Right*" anyway, and furthermore, that his chosen consort, SARPANIT, was a seventh generation descendent of *Adapa*, the hybrid man born from direct genetics of *Enki*, and therefore "Dragonblood." But the decree had been made. If it would not be *given* in order to reign on Earth in Babylon during his time—the *Age of Aries*—then "Divine Right" would have to be *taken*.

Contemporary archaeologists first became aware of the Babylonian "*Epic of Creation*" cycle in 1849, when cuneiform tablets were recovered during an expedition of the "Royal Library of Ashurbanipal" in *Nineveh*. Its contents were first published academically in 1876. They received significant attention from historians, mythographers and biblical scholars—not only because of their antiquity, but because of how significant the work turned out to be in deciphering the "methodology" of all ancient religions. In short—scholars discovered that the Babylonian "*Epic of Creation*" was the basis of the Judeo-Christian "*Book of Genesis*." But, after so many centuries of misinformation, *who would believe it?*

Multiple versions of the "*Enuma Eliš*" and other Mesopotamian creation-cycles exist but there is one key element that many esoteric practitioners and academic historians miss when appropriating origins for the tablets within the "bigger picture." All tablet-cycles making reference to "*Marduk*" at all, are purely *Babylonian*—not Sumerian. They reflect usurpation and transfer of "power" in Mesopotamia to *Babylon*, the control of the empire by priest-magicians and dragon-kings—authorities of religious and spiritual systems for the people and their relationship with the "Gods."

The usurpation was covert. Publicly, "Divine Right" *could* be demonstrated to coincide with the "World Order" decreed by *Anu, Enlil* and *Enki* in prehistoric times, *using* the *Enuma Eliš* to elevate *Marduk* and develop *Babylon* as the earthly seat of godly power!

ENUMA-ELIŠ : THE SEVEN TABLETS OF CREATION

I.

a.)—ABZU (*the Abyss*) and TIAMAT (*the Cosmic Dragon*) are first forms form the One (*All*).

b.)—Generations of "gods" are born and begin to make too much noise.

c.)—TIAMAT entrusts her vizier KINGU the power to fight for her.

d.)—TIAMAT creates calamity and a horde of monsters as ammunition.

II.

a.)—Enki reveals the plot against the gods to ANSAR.

b.)—A primary discourse from Tablet-I is repeated.

III.

a.)—Anu, Enlil and Enki do not stand fit to battle against TIAMAT.

b.)—Marduk is petitioned to champion the Anunnaki gods.

c.)—Marduk asks for supreme divinity if successful; to be *Chief God*.

IV.

a.)—The Anunnaki agree to Marduk's terms and prepare him for battle.

b.)—Marduk receives a "cloak of invisibility."

c.)—Marduk enchants his favored weapon: a bow.

d.)—Marduk destroys KINGU with a thunderbolt.

e.)—TIAMAT is slain; her minions are scattered and sent to "secret places."

f.)—Marduk fashions a "*Gate*" to seal these energies separate from the material universe

V.

a.)—Marduk seals the cosmic systems of "Lights," "Spheres" and "Degrees" under himself.

b.)—A material-matix *below* is fragmented by "seven," while the *heights* remain divided into "twelve."

c.)—The "*Anunnaki Star-Gate*" system is sealed throughout the Universe.

d.)—Marduk sets up a throne for himself next to Anu.

VI.

a.)—The Anunnaki praise Marduk for his feats.

b.)—The "Key to the Gate" (of the *Abyss* or *Dragon*) is "hidden" in genetic memory of the "*Race of Marduk*," including humans upgraded by Enki.

c.)—Babylonian systematization begins.

VII.

a.)—Having slayed TIAMAT and granted power over material creation, Marduk takes the names and numbers of Enlil.

b.)—Marduk takes the "signs" and
esoteric knowledge ("magic") of Enki.

c.)—Marduk fractures then seals all
systems on Earth under his name.

Politically, the *Enuma Eliš* allowed "*Laws of Marduk*" (for example, "*Hammurabi's Code*") and other Mardukite traditions to be upheld. In religious ceremonies—such as the Babylonian New Year "Akiti" Festival—the *Enuma Eliš* was part of preliminary the "rites" conducted in public. Any significant rituals, and even smaller operations of "magic" or "personal devotion" were typically "opened" with a recital of the *Epic* in validation of the Mardukite Tradition.

Words of the *Enuma Eliš* cement the basis of all *Mardukite* "*magic*"—a term used by anthropologists and esoteric practitioners of the Mardukite movement, but which the ancients simply viewed as "*Life*."

The older public ("exoteric") Sumerian *Epics of Creation* are hardly true creation "epics." Their systematic or quasi-cosmological basis is often restricted to a few opening lines, such as:

AN carries off heaven;
Enlil carries off earth.

To a purely pre-Babylonian "*Sumerian*" cosmology, this simplistic methodology simply *stood* by its own right unquestioned. Such simply *was* and had *always been*. To glean anything deeper, one would have had to become initiated to the "mystery tradition" observed by Babylonian magicians and scribes—the overseers of the "Realm" that supported the "*Dragon-Kings*" ruling by "Divine Right" of their "*dragon blood*" that originally "descended from the heavens"—from the "gods."

A more physical representation of the "*dragon*" also appears in *Babylon*, though surviving records are obscure. *Marduk* had two half-brothers (fathered by *Enki* but not necessarily born of *Ninki*)—*Ningiszida* (*Ningishzidda* or *Ni-(n)rah*) and *Ninazu* or *Tis(h)pak*. The famous "Dragon of Babylon" first belonged to *Tispak*, was later given to *Marduk* (as shown in popular artistic depictions) and eventually it came to to the care of *Nabu*. The best renderings are left left Nebuchadnezzar II in his construction of walls and gates of the Babylonian Renaissance.

The traditional name for the dragon name is *Sirius* or *Sirrus,* sometimes spelled phonetically as "*Sirush*" or "*Sirrush*." The Akkadian name for the species is *mushussu* or *mushhushshu*, meaning "furious serpent,"—from *mush-us,* or "monster." [This species should not be confused with the *usumgal*, or "Great Cosmic Serpent" used to represent the universe.] Far away in the African Congo, a description of the *mushussu* matches a species of *sauropod* (now believed to be extinct) called *mokele-mbembe* by the indigenous tribes who claimed to have killed one. This could effectively connect dragon-lore with the dinosaurs. Yet, where dragon-lore is universal, contemporary knowledge of dinosaurs has only been in public evidence for the last 200 years.

"Mastery of Dragons" has long-standing associations with *godhood* ever since these earliest renderings. Evidence still remains in Judeo-Christian lore: the *One God* was eventually seen as 'too great' to be concerned with mortal battle and so the 'dragon-slaying' motif was passed on to "ambassadors" or "emissaries" of God—first *St. Michael* (the archangel most closely associated with *Marduk*) and then among chosen mortals like *St. George*. Overt publicly visible possession of a live dragon as both a *royal pet* and *icon* of the holy city further led to securing a worldly "seat of god" for *Babylon* in the consciousness of the masses.

— 11 —

ANCIENT BABYLONIAN MAGIC
The Art of Magicians, Priests & Kings

"Systematic traditions, 'hermetically sealed'
within themselves, later rose from Semitic
grimoire-styled ceremonial magic, not
surprisingly influenced by 'Egypto-Babylonian'
forms of ritual magic—first the domain of Enki
and then Marduk and his scribe-son Nabu.
Priest-magicians of Babylon would not actually
have used 'grimoire-like' magic themselves.
This was not their way. At best, they invoked
the powers of the Anunnaki with incantations
in the name of Marduk—but the manner of
using 'secret names' as properties of Marduk,
or any other demigod, is a much more recent
addition to the Hermetic system."

~ Joshua Free, *Liber-R*

Under the banner of a *"New Age movement"* led
by *"esotericists,"* we are witnessing a revival of
pragmatic spiritual and ritualistic elements
drawn from ancient pagan and occult methodologies. We should be seeing no shortage of authentic Mesopotamian lore— being the origins
of all these later *systems*. But this information is
not readily accessible and esoteric success is not

achieved via pouring through a *kabbalastic grimoire* written by some *medieval sorcerer*. For this, the *seeker* will have to dig a little harder in the desert sands – into the heart of the true and authentic, antiquated and originating arts of the priests, magicians and kings!

During the era of the first *ziggurat* temples—the *Anunnaki* age—all "magic" constituted "spiritual assistance" governed by the state, ruled by priest-kings and temple attendants. All official "mystics" of *Babylonia* were employed by the temples and scribe-houses. There were undoubtedly many others with access to esoteric knowledge who confined themselves to their arts in the *outlands*, beyond the awareness of the societal "realm." The "common" class in Mesopotamia, however, did not really practice "magic" in the way it is generally classified by anthropologists. Personal religious devotions were primarily composed of *hymns* and *prayers* learned from the temples.

Cuneiform tablets describing "magical" ceremonies list required religious artifacts and items that the average person would not have access to or the ability to afford. "*Magic*" from this period is restricted to the priests. Use of a temple, for one, appears key—a tradition continued among some modern *lodges* of "ceremonial magic." Access to tablets themselves—records and *"incantation-prayers"* maintained directly by the priests—was not generally given to just anyone. And you had to be able to read them and memorize them. General collections of these tablets were seldom kept, except priest-kings maintaining their own personal libraries. According to *Mardukite Tablet-B*:—

> *"The priest is to observe pious ways, and Rites of Offering at the Altar of Sacrifice. This is performed by intoning prayers [incantations] from tablets in conjunction with offering of incense, grain [bread], honey [with butter] and libations of buttermilk (or wine). Sacred "holy" oil [and water] make an appearance in virtually all ancient Babylonian rites—water and oil frequently placed in bowls before icons [of deities] in temples, in addition to offerings of alabaster, gold and lapis lazuli."*

At the temple-shrines, the Altar of Offering was set before the *"Boat of the Gods."* The same imagery appears in Egyptian Tradition—a "Boat

---

* Refer to *"The Complete Anunnaki Bible"* or *"Necronomicon: The Anunnaki Bible"* edited by Joshua Free.

of the Gods" carrying seven figures, *e.g.* the *Seven Anunnaki Gods* of the Babylonian "Younger Generation." Smaller personal altars could surely be constructed by a devotee appealing to their *god*, but became more prominent with the rise of "*figurative mysticism*," because originally, these offerings would be physically received by a *god*, or via their "priestly secretaries." Common religious offerings included food and drink, incense and oil, even lavish jewelry and clothing, all of which were carried up the *ziggurat* steps—up the "*ladder to heaven*"—to be placed before the feet of the *god*. When the *gods*, themselves, were not present, it was customary to have an *official* piece of statuary left in their place. Thus, it is easy to see how these original activities evolved into later *magical* and *religious* practices.

White was the most common color worn by the priests, although black was also used and even favored by the temple-priestesses. Priestly attire included the infamous "conical hat," popularly associated today with classical "wizards," but which can be seen worn by *gods*, kings and priest-magicans in ancient Mesopotamia, Egypt and eventually elsewhere. Gold and *lapis lazuli* commonly appear as both "magical ritual aids" and prestigious offerings to the gods. Babylonian temples and sacred structures were often designed to radiate these hues. Wands, necklaces and carried bags of loose *lapis lazuli* are often mentioned on esoteric tablets, in addition to golden rings and "amulet-plates" marked with specific seals and cuneiform glyphs.

Modern implementation of a "practical magical system" based on the "Mardukite" Babylonian paradigm is different than what the contemporary mind—even an "*esoteric*" one—is fundamentally familiar with. As opposed to later magicians who appear to have had to connive and fool hierarchies of spirits into assisting them, threatening them and even in fear of some retroactive revenge, the original magical system used by priests of *Babylonia* was rooted in a deep personal relationship of "authority" with the cosmos. Scribes maintained the "sources" of not only their religious power, but a fundamental system of civilization promoting progression of the human species into today. All of this, according to tradition, rested in the power of the *Anunnaki gods*—and the priest-kings and scribes were installed to be sure this was never forgotten.

— 12 —

ANUNNAKI STAR-GATES OF BABYLON
The Divine Power of "StarFire"

*"True indeed, there was a supreme name
which possessed the power of commanding the
gods and extracting from them a perfect
obedience, but that name remained the
inviolable secret of Enki. In exceptional cases
the priest besought Enki, through the mediator
Marduk, to pronounce the solemn word in order
to reestablish order in the world and restrain
the powers of the Abyss. But the priest did not
know that name, and could not in consequence
introduce it into his formulae. He could not
obtain or make use of it, he only requested the
god who knew it to employ it, without endeavor-
ing to penetrate the terrible secret himself."*

~ M. Lenormant, *Chaldean Magic & Sorcery*

Compared to a relatively more recent world of
"magical" folk traditions—where love potions
are in no short supply and acquisition of cosmic
favor is just a matter of spinning around seven
times while whistling or throwing feathers to
the north winds—the original stoic and sacred
rites of "divine magic" are rooted in a "mystical" tradition based on a direct relationship, and

personal "authority" *earned*, with the *Anunnaki gods*. The mere existence of an ancient "Anunnaki hierarchy" produced the later mystical and religious concept of "*spiritual pantheons*"— pantheons cataloged by *kabbalistic magicians* in later attempts to uncover the "secret of the ages," or more specifically, the secret "*magic word*" that granted authority with the *forces* of the *cosmos*.

In regards to modern "Mardukite" revivals by any practitioner or group—since such cultural revisits are common in "New Age" mystical paradigms—the *specific* ancient ideology or paradigm represented in this book should be kept in mind, particularly if interested in practicing "meditations" or metaphysical experiments. Connecting effective esoteric knowledge —*one-to-one*—with physical representations or graphic is another common aspect of mysticism. For example, lacking access to the shrines of Babylon or physical *ziggurat* temples, a modern practitioner employs "creative visualization," advanced "meditation" techniques, or other methods of "spirit travel" to connect with the same "energetic forces." The *Anunnaki* specifically, are not necessarily the "UFO-driving aliens" heard of today. There are many other factions of life in the universe interested in humans and planet Earth. However, the *Anunnaki* are very powerful beings who made such deep impressions on the "Akashic Field" that their identities still remain accessible today.

Modern psychology, quantum physics, and practical mysticism all suggest that the energetic self does not properly distinguish a reality barrier between what it encounters or experiences in the body as "day-to-day" from what is possible in properly executed ritual drama. In ancient times, the priests reinforced cultural beliefs in society through dramatic reenactments of ancient myths, thereby making them part of "day-to-day" social consciousness—allowing for this "*magic*" to become *reality*. All of it, of course, *really* being a matter of *perspective*. For whatever we may attribute to our "accomplishments of things," it is our belief that we can execute them that makes anything possible.

The Babylonian "Religio-Magic" System was developed by ancient *Mardukites* as a means of sealing power of an older generation of *gods* under *Marduk*—with his holding a "*kingship*" over the "younger generation" of *Anunnaki* that served devotional needs of post-Sumerian *Babylonia*. Thus, cosmic power was accessed *through him* and worldly power was dispatched *by him*. And, so long as they could be honored within the confines of the prescribed system, "Enlilite" figures such as *Inanna* (*Ishtar*), *Nergal* (*Erra*), *Nanna* (*Sin*) and *Shammash/Samas* (*Uttu*) and *Ninurta* (*Ninib*) all appear within this "younger pantheon" observed by *Mardukites*, even if they are *not* descendents of *Enki*. "*Sealing*" this *system* in Babylon is what caused the city-name to be interpreted literally as the "*Gate of the Gods*"—"*bab*" (as "gateway") and "*ilu*" (meaning, "god," "star" or "heaven").

"Gateways" appear as an archetypal theme at the heart and soul of all esoteric "religion" and "spirituality" born in Mesopotamia; thereafter, those treating "Gates of Heaven." When confronted with "divine" matters—or that which is *otherworldly* (pertains to the "*other*")—"Gate" symbolism is nearly always present. As the mind perceives it, "*gates*" are "thresholds," "portals," "doorways" and "windows" into what is "*Other*"—what is *beyond* our preset daily awareness. "*Arcane Tablets*"* suggest there is only *one* reality—one existence in wholeness— but fragmented (from our point of view) into arbitrary parts via these "veils," "levels," "layers" and other "boundaries" of existence and awareness.

---

* See also "*The Tablets of Destiny*" by Joshua Free.

Since the 1970's practical efforts have been made toward modern revival of a "Mardukite" Babylonian "Gatekeeping" (or "Gatewalking") tradition under a guise of "*Necronomicon.*" But most lore is from ancient literature describing an era of history when priests and magicians worked alongside *Anunnaki gods* in establishing and preserving physical *gates* and *shrines.* These structures clearly served multiple purposes in the ancient paradigm, both those that were known to the population—and those unknown.

Following in the pious footsteps of *Babylonian priests,* whether a modern *seeker* or revivalist *practitioner* has been truly *self-honestly* dedicated to the *system* or not, the primordial power of these currents, to be useful or channeled directly—must be first respected. This path, if it is to be applied today, requires cumulatively developed "spiritual authority" developed from working with the archetypal currents of this pantheon with "techniques" dating back to a ancient time of kings, priests and magicians.

The "*magic,*" then—if we are to call it that— comes directly from a *working* relationship between the individual (priest or magician) and the "powers" controlling the specified domains. In the ancient world, all facets of life were thought to be the domain or under the influence of some "unseen" force—but a force that could be understood and communicated with through magic and religion. This led to the solidification of civilized humans under a "world order"—but one that was transmutable and subject to additional programming and control.

For modern purposes, the term *"Gatekeeping"* or *"Gatewalking"* really applies to the "Mardukite" (*Babylonian*) specific method of *kabbalistic* "pathwork"—predating and serving as origins for the more commonly known Semitic *"Kabbalah"* (or "Cabala"). The methodology is used today by modern *"Mardukite Zuism"* and *"Mardukite Systemology"*—those who actively participate in a revival of ancient *Mardukite* wisdom and paradigms as it applies to Life, Reality and Universes.

Where a temple is not accessible, *"magic carpets"* and *"statuary"* can be set out to consecrate an area for *priestly magic*. Ritual texts often refer to an *"image of your god and goddess"* and/or displaying a line of *"seven winged figures,"* indicative of the "Younger Generation." As in modern traditions, ritual space (outside of the temple) is observed as a *mandala* or "sacred circle." Representing ceremony and agriculture, the boundary of a circle was originally marked by consecrated *"flour of Nisaba"*—or the *"flour of Nabu,"* as Babylonian tradition evolved. This is performed the same way a modern *"ceremonialist"* might draw theirs ritual circle in chalk, &tc.

As advice to the priest or magician, the *Tablet-Q Series* (in *"The Complete Anunnaki Bible"*) offers this step:—

> *"Make your invocation to Marduk and Sarpanit. Then call in [invoke] the Supernal Trinity—Anu, Enlil and Enki, followed by a conjuration [consecration] of the Fire and Four Beacons [lamps] of the Watchtowers [cardinal directions]. Perform the 'Incantation of Eridu' and call forth the presence of your personal sedu [guardian watcher spirit]."*

Using mystical conjuration to summon a "personal watcher-spirit" is part of the most ancient beliefs; not exclusive to Egypto-Babylonian or *Hermetic* systems. The *sedu* ("spirit," "genius" or "intelligence," much like the Greek word *"daemon"*) is the origin of a traditional Assyrian concept, later more commonly known as a "guardian angel." According to Babylonian beliefs, every person *had* one. This belief may not have been shared by all since lines from some of the older incantations are requests to initially "acquire" a *sedu* and a *lamassu*. In either case, we are presented with a "magic" that carries a strength dependent on one's own true understanding and personal relationship with the cosmos.

There are many types of "beings" in the universe, the *Anunnaki* are only one—perhaps the first—to engineer reality for humans on Earth. These "angelic" traditions become more mysterious as they evolved. Identities of IGIGI-"Watcher" spirits fade when contrasted to a host of other forces in existence—some seeming *malignant*. In ancient Mesopotamia, the "Demonic Spirits" that humans required protection from were often resonance of pestilence and warfare. Most ancient *taboo*-sins or "*bans*"—found listed on various tablets—were meant to keep people clean and free of infections and disease. Laws were put forth to keep civility, without people having to murder or resort to eating one another.

Regimens of personal cleanliness were essential among the priest and magician class—not only in their conductance of ceremony, but in their everyday walking lives as well. Keeping hair trimmed, or even shaved, was a part of daily ritual—it aided in thwarting personal insect infestations. Use of eye makeup, once thought to be purely decorative, actually had some evolutionary advantages for desert living. Black eyeshadow, particularly beneath the eyes (as used by today's athletes) assists in reducing the sunglare common to open sandy areas.

"Divine Names" play a key role in both ancient and modern magical or priestly (mystic) work. Sometimes several "names" or mythic "titles" for the same entity are invoked. Even the priest-magician must proposition the *gods* by properly introducing himself with recitation of his lineage. For example, "*I, so-and-so, the son of so-and-so and so-and-so, whose god and goddess is so-and-so and so-and-so. . .*" All of the spoken words involved are really, then, quite direct. *Who are you? Who are you calling? What is the message?*—Just as if you are dealing with a *Divine Secretary*, and yes, the Babylonians even installed Nabu and Teshmet to this real position! The system is very "formal."

Keep in mind that the entire effectiveness of the priest's magical work was based on their personal relationship with the *gods*—not simply their ability to discern a *secret number* or precisely memorize an *incantation formula*. These later "magical" beliefs evolved more recently as the *gods* seemed to become more distant from our world.

Original ritualized *petitions* for "divine" assistance seem more akin to requesting help from a *friend* or *authority*. There is a certain measure of *tact* involved, perhaps once common knowledge, that later developed as "occult correspondences." In this case—*This one is only home after 5. That one is more content around the smell of roses. Offer to take this one to lunch first. Mondays are NOT that one's day! &tc. &tc.* How often is this true of our own "Judicial System" even today? Those who made this work their everyday lives in the temples generally knew this type of information, particularly in regards to their own patron deities. Circulation of "*grimoires,*" *prayerbooks* or unauthorized "*spellbooks*" among the masses began as the system evolved from those "outside" the ranks of the national tradition—from those not even sworn to its sanctity.

Secrets of the "Ancient Mystery School" are not dependent on widespread dispersion for them to exist—the *Power* and *Knowledge* is there for *any* that choose to *Seek* it.

— 13 —

INTRODUCING MARDUKITE MAGIC
The Ancient Rites & Rituals of Eridu

*"Through Marduk, the power of Eridu—incant-
ation-prayer and "intention"—was taught to
the scribes of Nabu and the Mardukite Priests,
who were taught to attract and compel the
'gods' in the name of Marduk, always incanting
the word-formula of the highest order: Nabu
invoked by way of the name of Marduk;
Marduk invoked by way of the name of Enki,
Our Father, who in turn would invoke by the
name of Anu—and so was born the concept of
magical hierarchies, an ideal that was
convoluted and obscured when employed later
(during the Middle Ages and such), particularly
distorted by the Judeo-Christian paradigm as
evident in many popular grimoires"*

~ Joshua Free, *Book of Marduk*

A modern seeker interested in esoteric philosophies has undoubtedly found countless
"primers" and "handbooks" of magic and sorcery or other ritual "grimoires." Many contemporary guides employ "creative visualization"
and "New Thought" techniques—the same ones
used by popular self-help gurus and motivation-

al mentors—as well as other forms of meditation, conscious breathing, mental concentration or focus of will. These methods are actually quite effective in the right hands. The material world experienced by an individual is subject to that person's own "energies" and perspective (internal "set") in addition to their interactions with other "energies." Nonetheless, physical "ceremony" is often sought as a necessary step in crossing the thresholds of our own psyche.

Many versions of "*Erudite*" magic are found throughout Mesopotamian "religio-spiritual" (or "magical") cuneiform tablets. Incantations used in the "Mardukite Babylonian Anunnaki Tradition"—from those tablets forged by priest-scribes of the *Order of Nabu*—are actually invoked from the "perspective" ("*authority*") of *Nabu*. This reflects how the tradition was learned verbatim from *Marduk*.

Both scholarly and esoteric texts concur that the "Opening Ritual" for *Mardukite* magic originates with a rite called—"*The Incantation of Eridu*." It is perhaps the most fundamental "formula" of the magical system in *Babylonia*. It returns one's focus to the heart of the *system* and the roles of its main *figures*—*Nabu* as Director, and the appropriation of his father, Marduk as the "Chief." This is what is acknowledged in the

"*Incantation of Eridu*," also known as the "*Incantation of the Deep*," alluding to another name for the far-away abode of *Enki* near the *Persian Gulf*.

Ceremonial "affirmations" activate the "*covenant*" of Anunnaki power sealed in *Eridu*, and then in *Babylon*. This allows a practitioner to assume a representative "*god-form*" as the "*Priest of Eridu*"—a title first bestowed upon *Marduk* by *Enki* in the Sumerian age, then passed onto *Nabu* during standardization of the *Babylonian* era. An esoteric key is in effect here. The priest conducts the "incantations" ("ceremony") as an embodiment of the intermediary "messenger" *deity*. This is the original meaning of the word "*invocation*." The priest is *not* "evoking" or "conjuring" some apparition—he is directing the flow of *Cosmic Order* by calling specific personality energies "into" *himself*.

The magician is *approaching* his deity as himself—*a servant priest*—and petitions to assume the *godform*, whereby he continues the ceremony as a *divine representation* of the invoked *god*. Similar principles appear in Semitic mysticism and the Judeo-Kabbalah. An an excellent ceremonial example is found in contemporary Catholicism, when the priest "*assumes a Christ-*

form" to effectively perform "alchemical trans-mutation" on the sacramental bread and wine. He conducts this rite as a representative of Jesus on earth, an imitative ritual drama, reenacting the "Last Supper." In the "Mardukite" system observed in *Babylon*, the god invoked is typically Marduk. This is affirmed with the priest's first utterance of—"*It is not I, but Marduk, who speaks the incantation*"—activating and sealing the Mardukite Mystical System for "practical" and "religious" use.

Consider the lines of this incantation, adapted for the Mardukite "*Conjuration of the Fire God*" from *Tablet-Y* series:—

> *It is not I, but Marduk, Slayer of Serpents,*
> *Who summons thee.*
> *It is not I, but Enki, Father of the Magicians,*
> *Who calls thee here now.*

As previously introduced, the ritual operates from the perspective ("*authority*") of Nabu, speaking for Marduk. Many variations of this rite exist, including several Assyrian "exorcisms." As an example, one of these cuneiform tablets, translated by R.C. Thompson, relates the opening lines:—

The Priest of E.A. [Enki] am I.
The priest of Damkina [Ninki] am I.
The messenger [Nabu] of Marduk am I.
My spell is the spell of E.A [Enki].
My incantation is the incantation of Marduk.
The 'magic circle' of EA [Enki] is in my
*   hand.*
The 'tamarask' of Anu, in my hand, I hold.

Opening lines from the modern *Mardukite* version in *Tablet-Y* read:—

I am the Priest of Marduk,
Son of Our Father, Enki.
I am the Priest of Eridu,
And the Magician of Babylon.

The Assyrian version continues as follows:—

EA [Enki], King of the Deep
See me favorably.
I, the magician, am thy slave.
March thou on my right hand,
Assist me on my left;
Add thy pure spell to mine.
Add thy pure voice to mine.
O god that blesses me, Marduk,
Let me be blessed, wherever my path rests.
Thy power, shall god and man proclaim.
And I too, the magician, thy slave.

E.A. Budge translated an older version for
"*Babylonian Life & History*," where we see another Mardukite method for petitioning the
"younger pantheon" of Anunnaki to the side of
the priest:—

> *I am the Priest of EA [Enki].*
> *I am the Magician of Eridu.*
> *Samas [Shammash] is before me.*
> *Nanna [Sin] is behind me.*
> *Nergal is at my right hand.*
> *Ninurta is at my left hand.*

Adding to this, the modern *Mardukite* version
appends:—

> *Anu, above me, King of Heaven.*
> *Enki, below me, King of the Deep.*
> *The power [blood] of Marduk is within me.*
> *It is not I, but Marduk,*
> *Who performs the incantation.*

A priest mystically sheds awareness of their
"mortal spark," even if only for a moment—to
experience "*transcendental magic*" clad in *godhood*. Direct parallels may be drawn from this
rite to others found in "Hermetic" magic and the
"Kabbalah." Rising on the planes of perception,
awareness and knowing—as a *god*, speaking on
behalf of the *Chief* of the pantheon—the magic-

ian-priest is now able to influence worldly affairs in the *original* and most powerfully direct "magical" means known—a direct interface with the *gods* as one of their own.

THE MAGIC OF BABYLON

APPENDIX

OF LIBER-51

*A collection of esoteric supplements
released alongside Liber-51 and
as an Appendix in former editions.*

EPILOGUE

"A Brave New Babylon Rising"
by David Zibert

Conflict. . . Unrest. . .
  On earth as it is in heaven. . .
At the precipice of a planetary evolution,
  the *world* ends.
    It always does. . .

Global tensions rise to unprecedented heights with the passing of each day. The *bright future* once wrought for mankind grows dark for the race as a whole. To it: arcane philosophy failed; ageless religion failed; humanistic ideals failed; and every magic spell and scientific formulae furthers sealing mortal man in his own self-made systematic prison, driving the coffin nail home—a single-track to travel upon furthering our journey into the *downward spiral* sending a world into inevitability. . .

                    . . .apocalypse.

And this is my hope for the world, shared from the depth of my soul and joined in the voices of many self-honest truth seekers who have seen for themselves. . . renewal!

Mystics know; children know; even *birds* know—the world is *ending*. Of course, this does not imply blatant physical, material and totalitarian destruction of humans (so let us not employ the same scare tactics of every evangelizing preacher under the sun), it is instead the ending of *a human world*.

Recorded legends on ancient tablets point toward an era of *renewal* that will give way to the fabled *Golden Age*, a *Brave New World*—a true *new age*. But this is no *new* idea at all, rather it is something predicted by the main tenets of every true spiritual path throughout history, differentiated solely by semantics and appearing as varied as opinions from the *Second Coming of Christ* to the the cosmic collapse of the material universe by some rift in space-time or even *dark matter* and *black holes*.

You can label and interpret, even sugarcoat, what is happening any way you like—the simple fact remains: There is an undeniable feeling shared throughout the collective human consciousness that *something* is about to happen—that something *is* happening—and yet it all seems to endlessly cycle back and forth in some determined fragile balance... So *what* are we to do?

While the bungled confusion of the world plagues the mind with anxiety demons and victimization tendencies, the answer couldn't be simpler: *we must provoke the end of the world*, in this case, through a *massive paradigm shift*, meaning the necessary return of the *true spirituality*. By this, I mean the original *stuff*; untainted; undefiled through time by the analytical minds and personal truths of men corrupted into *systems*—fragmented from the whole; never the tween shall meet; *thank you, call back later*. It may seem like nothing new; but *no*, this time *it is different*.

In the wake of this self-honest planetary need for a *Great Awakening*, and on the cusp of a true *new age*, many "cults" have risen in recent past, loosely termed "pagan." Yet, in all of their once revolutionary efforts marked upon human consciousness, what they have to offer is often really only a "turn of the wheel," simply providing a different container for the *same content*, proving to us once again that humanity has not evolved much since the days of antiquity.

Understand we are not here to tell you what to think, raising our "*Mardukite literature*" to some new authoritarian heights, but we are offering critical information and data correction for your noggin so that you might *self-honestly* think for *yourself*. The emphasis here on *self* is not merely some glorification of individualism or newfangled ego-worship, but an affirmation that if we really want to change the *world*, we had better clean up and change our *self* first.

When each human being takes the responsibility to grasp the *self-honest* realizations of who they are and where they come from, what the world is and how it was made, of the stuff dreams and stars are made of, the *universe* and *everything*—when the experience of all these things can be done *honestly* from *self*, then the race will see an end to the current melancholy, heinous nonsense that is happening and has been happening for quite some time— a condition that is actually *anathema* to the survival of the very creatures that keep these things the way they are!

The premises we use to chart a *new world* are simple enough:

- *Every* human being has the potential and responsibility to experience life in *self-honesty.*

- *Every* human being has the right and freedom to demand this of their existence.

- *Every* human being has to embrace *some universal oneness* in order to live in harmony with itself as a race of brethren; with the Earth as a base of homestead; and with the universe as a matrix of existence. Only then can humans experience true *unity with all life, the universe and everything!*

This is our *true* and *destined* existence.

But what has kept man from achieving these ends? Why is it that the shortcomings of humanity throughout history seem to keep repeating recursively? Why has *everything* failed? As with all else, we find that the answer is again quite simple: *because humans are forgetful*. We forget easily; we are often sad; we suffer; we lose sight. To regain anything meaningful for the present and any hope for the future, we must remember what once was, and fortunately for us, an order of some of the earliest mystics thought of just that—so they created *cuneiform-writing*.

This book, as with the remaining "cycle" of literature produced by the *"Mardukites,"* is sure to present to you ideas of "history" and "magic" in ways you have never seen, or maybe even imagined before. The tradition that it represents does not deal in rudimentary hierarchical *grimoires* or the application of general hermetic principles upon some historical ethnocentric tradition. The "Mardukite" work runs much deeper than even this. It presents *The System*—the *archetypal* system—that has formed the basis for every mystery tradition to later emerge.

In other words: if you can correctly understand the means and motives of the mysteries and religion of Babylon and Sumer, you will correctly be able to interpret "history" and "magic" as a whole— whatever these words may mean to you. You will become privy to the beauty of the original efforts that have mostly deteriorated with time, probably attaining its lowest evolutionary depths in Christian-controlled medieval Europe – or even in the practices of modern day Jews and Muslims who use religion to shroud political reasons for killing one another. Even more important perhaps, you will become aware of what *really* happened in ancient Babylon, and understand whether or not it really was the *right* way to execute *Divine Order*, and why.

Indeed—the focal point of the modern *Mardukite* movement has never been about bringing back the *verbatim* "Babylonian paradigm" one-to-one, because this would only be the "turn of the wheel" again, and we've already grown dizzy and tired by such ventures. *This time*, it's all about fixing what went wrong, actually fixing the problem of *systems*, the root of all problems really, at the core. When every individual takes up the *Sword of Truth* against the world, executing the *acid test* of *self-honesty* on reality, then no doubt a *new*, better, *upgraded* aeon will really begin for mankind. This, we call: *New Babylon!*

To those who *also* feel called to pursue this with us, we say:

WELCOME HOME!

DICTIONARY OF ANUNNAKI GODS

ADAD {10}—The youngest son of ENLIL that becomes the national patron deity to the *Hittites* (called HADAD or TESHUB); possibly also recognized as BAAL HADAD in a *Hittite* version of the Supernal Trinity that is elevated to a chief god position in the same manner that MARDUK is raised in *Babylon*. As a storm god in the Anunnaki pantheon, ADAD is represented by thunder, lightning and torrents. According to Hittite records, succession of hierarchical kingship passes from ALALU to ANU to KUMARBI (ENLIL) and then BA'AL HADAD (TESHUB). In the Enki'ite (Mardukite) Babylonian system he is named ISHKUR and granted the position of "*Inspector of the Cosmos*" by ENKI.

ALALU ["*Father of the Gods*"]—The figure maintaining 'kingship' in the 'heavens' prior to ANU. An ancient *Hittite* (*Hurrian*) tablet cycle titled ALALU & ANU or "*Kingship in Heaven*" describes a conflict between the two for the seat of 'kingship' in the 'heavens'. The Mardukite *Tablet-K* series reprinted in "*The Anunnaki Bible*" explains: Formerly in the Ancient of Days, ALULU was reigning in heaven; and for nine *sars* did he rule the skies, but not well did he reign. Then in the ninth *sar* of his reign, ANU defeated ALULU. ALULU descended from heaven and ruled the dark-hued earth. ANU gave fight and defeated

ALULU and kingship was lowered from heaven to earth by decree of ANU.

ALULU *see* ALALU

ASAR(I)LUHI *see* MARDUK

AMARUTU *see* MARDUK

AN/ANSAR *see* ANU

ANTU {55} [*"Life of Heaven"*]—The official half-sister (by a different mother) and spouse (consort) of ANU. ANTU and ANU beget ENLIL. In archaic pre-*Sumerian* lore, ANTU is espoused to the archaic AN.

ANUNITUM *see* INANNA

ANU {60} [*"Heavenly One"*]—In the *Sumerian* Anunnaki patheon, ANU is the supreme *"All-Father"* of the pantheon; father to ENLIL by official spouse ANTU, and the father of ENKI & NINHURSAG (by other wives). Called AN in pre-*Babylonian* times and ANU by the *Babylonians*, a being whose family resides on, or emerged from the 'place of crossings' (*Nibiru*). Few of the incantation tablets (or 'prayers') invoke the powers of ANU directly, since the "heavenly force" was perceived as too vast to be channeled in its raw state, and to degrade it to anything more accessible would be to compromise the nature of what is being represented by this figure.

ANZU ["*Knower of Heaven*"]—An obscure bird-like beast/monster of an unclear nature. The ANZU or ZU usually refers to a "heavenly bird" or thunderbird that appears in an archaic tab-let cycle stealing the '*Tablets of Destiny*" from EN-LIL, disrupting the DUR-AN-KI ('Bond-Heaven-Earth') "stargate." It is possible that this half-man, half-bird, sometimes called AZAG, was a genetically engineered storm-god or artificially intelligent messenger being of ENLIL that turned "evil."

ARURU—The sister of ENLIL, alias NINTU, who is the *Babylonian* title for the 'mother-goddess' known in *Sumerian* as NINMAH or NIN-HURSAG. In the Babylonian ethnocentric epics, she assists MARDUK in creating the human race (or '*Race of Marduk*'), however, in the *Enuma Elis*, it is "blood" of KINGU that is used. Other *Sumerian* versions say the "blood" or "essence" of some other 'slain' god is used for this.

AYA ["*Dawn*"]—The official spouse (consort) of SAMAS in *Akkadian*; named SHERIDA in *Sumerian*.

AZAG *see* ANZU

BAU ["*To Accompany*"]—A daughter of ANU, who is the official spouse (consort) to NINURTA in the pre-*Babylonian* (*Sumerian*) pantheon. Her names GULA ("*Big One*") and BAU (the sound a dog makes) are, perhaps idioms about her size/appearance. She remains a goddess in the *Babylonian* pantheon of healing (as NINTI-NUGGA).

BEL *see* EL

BUZUR *see* ENKI

DAMKINA *see* NINKI

DAMUZU *see* DUMUZI

DUMUZI ["*Son Who is Life*"]—Youngest son of ENKI and DUTTUR (a concubine of ENKI) who is the betrothed spouse (consort) to INANNA (ISHTAR) after MARDUK declines the tradition of espousing INANNA. DAMUZI is a shepherd god (as opposed to a grain deity), known as TAMMUZ in the Semitic languages. In the *Sumerian* version of the descent-cycle, INANNA descends to the *Underworld* in hopes of being its queen. When captured, she becomes a prisoner of her sister ERESHKIGAL and leaves to find someone to take her place. Upon returning to ERECH, she finds that DUMUZI has been celebrating his ascent to her throne and is not mourning for her death. Enraged, she immediately hands him over to the 'demons' of the *Underworld*. Later versions of this cycle depict the god MARDUK as somehow responsible for the death of DUMUZI and INANNA (ISHTAR) descends to the *Underworld* to release him.

EA *see* ENKI

EL—A Semitic form of the Akkadian (*Babyloni-an*) ILU or ILI, meaning '*Lofty Ones*', '*High Ones*' or '*Great Gods*'; the plural form being ILANI (or ELANI in *European Elvish-Faerie* lore), with a Semitic plural equivalent "*Elohim*", meaning liter-ally 'gods' but often used to denote the 'One God' in the Judeo-Christian *Old Testament* (which is, it-self, rooted strongly in Mesopotamian traditions). EL or BEL is also used to denote the 'Lord of the Earth-Space', or else 'ENLIL-SHIP', a position attributed not only to ENLIL (in the *Enlilite Sumerian* tradition) but also to NINURTA, MAR-DUK and even other patron deities by localized Middle Eastern cults. Later Semitic use of EL as a suffix (e.g., Micha*el*, Gabri*el*, etc.) matches the prefix use of the ILU sign in cuneiform, meaning "*Of God.*" In cuneiform, the sign is a "cross" and in later religious scriptures and rites, the literary tradition remained to place a cross before a *Divine* or saint name.

ELLIL *see* ENLIL

ENKI {40} "*Lord of the Earth*"—also known as E.A. ["*Whose Home is Water*"], firstborn son of ANU (but not the official heir), half-brother to ENLIL (heir of ANU). Also called NUDIMMUD (or PTAH in *Egypt*) meaning: "*The Fashioner*" (or "*Grand Designer*"). ENKI is the Chief scientist of the Anunnaki, taking up residence in *Eridu*, near the *Persian Gulf* and also in *Africa* (particularly *Egypt*). ENKI is father of MARDUK, begot with NINKI (DAMKINA) and is representative of the planet Neptune in the local Anunnaki 'world order'. ENKI is given control of the '*Waters of Life*' on Earth. He seeks to save his own ('*Mardukite*') legacy during the deluge and then is responsible for programing the arts and sciences of civilization into humanity. In later *Enlilite*-derived Judeo-Christian interpretations, ENKI becomes demon-ized as 'Satan'.

ENLIL {50} "*Lord of Air-Space*"—The official heir-son of ANU, '*Lord of the Command*' on Earth, revered as the '*God*' of Earth by Enlilite *Sumerians* and later derived Semitic (Hebrew) tradtions. EN-LIL begets his own heir, NINURTA, by his half-sister NINHURSAG, but espouses SUD, renamed NINLIL and begets NANNA. In the pre-*Babyloni-an* paradigm, ENLIL is the Jupiter position in the pantheon that is later usurped by MARDUK. *Sumerian* tradition observes ENLIL as the 'Father' to the Anunnaki pantheon, much in the same way that ENKI is revered by the *Mardukites*. Prominent descendents of ENLIL include: NANNA, SAMAS, INANNA and NERGAL in addition to NINURTA.

ENSAG *see* NABU

ENSHAG *see* NABU

ERESHKIGAL – ["*Mistress of the Great Below*"] The Queen of the *Great Lands* in the *Sumerian* tradition, sister of INANNA-ISHTAR, granddaughter of ENLIL and spouse to NERGAL.

ERRA *see* NERGAL

GANZIR — The gatekeeper to the underworld 'Kingdom of Shadows.' The '*Gate of Ganzir*' is often confused with the '*Gate to the Abyss*' or the '*Gate to the Outside*', but instead it is a portal into the Anunnaki-controlled *Underworld*, the '*Shadowlands*' or twilight world within the domain of ERESHKIGAL, who rules this 'land of the dead'. Quoting a modern grimoire of Babylonian occultism, the "necromantic art, by which is it desirous to speak with the phantom of someone dead, and perhaps dwelling in the ABSU [*Abyss*] and thereby a servant of ERESHKIGAL... it is no less than the opening of the *Gate of Ganzir*."

GIBIL ["*He Who Has Fire*"]—The companion of the flame, a descendent of ENKI who uses fire to conduct alchemy and other feats of "*fire power*."

GIRRA—The "servant", "power" or "fire" of the 'great god'; the *Sumerian* fire-god or essence or force of a fire-god named GIBIL.

GULA *see* BAU

HADAD *see* ADAD

ILLIL *see* ENLIL

ILU *see* EL

IMDUGUD *see* ANZU

INANNA {15} ["*Lady of Heaven*"]—The *Sumerian* goddess of "passion", both 'love' and 'war', and patron of URUK, begot by NANNA and NINGAL; originally betrothed to MARDUK, she then changes her consort choice to DUMUZI. Her prowess and determination secured her a place in all ancient pantheons; being the "*Goddess of One-Thousand Names*," titled ISHTAR in *Babylon*. INANNA (ISHTAR) is the spirit of Venus, whose day is Friday and with an essence found in copper. Her colors are green and white, significant to her domain of fertility and growth. She offers her magicians the skills in love and visions of beauty.

IRRA *see* NERGAL

ISHKUR *see* ADAD

ISHTAR *see* INANNA

KUR *see* TIAMAT

MAMMI *see* NINHURSAG

MARDUK {10/(50)} "*Son of God*"—The supreme champion of the IGIGI during the pre-

Sumerian era of the Anunnaki; heir-son of ENKI, he becomes the patron of *Babylon* and the 'Mardukite' tradition reigning for the *Age of Aries* in Mesopotamia. All tablet cycles making reference to MARDUK are purely *Babylonian* or from a direct later source, as he does not appear in any significant pre-Babylonian cuneiform tablet cycles yet unearthed. When mentioned briefly as the son of ENKI, working in *Eridu*, he is named AS-ARLUHI, becoming the patron Anunnaki "deity" of magic or 'Master of Magicians'after having inherited the craft from his father. The blatant industrious and expansive power represented by MARDUK in his ascent up the pantheon (as observed in *Babylon*) is typified by the planet Jupiter (ENLIL, by *Sumerian* standards). His color is purple.

MERIDUG *see* MARDUK

MERODACH *see* MARDUK

NABAK *see* NABU

NABIH *see* NABU

NABU {12} ["*Prophet*"]—The official post-*Sumerian* secretary of the Anunnaki, part-divine earth born heir-son of MARDUK and messenger-herald and spokesperson of the '*Mardukite*' tradition, the national cult of *Babylon* devised by NABU who assisted his father in the redevelopment of the Anunnaki paradigm (as seen in the

'*Mardukite*' religion of *Babylon* replacing the previously observed '*Enlilite*' world order of the *Sumerians*). Creating the concept of 'history' and 'propaganda', NABU gives the 'stylus' to humanity (and launches a group of scribe-priests (specially taught writing and rhetoric) to catalog the natures, identities, history and decrees (decisions) of the Anunnaki Assembly (gods) and their relationship with each other and the human ("mortal") world, thereby creating not only the first public 'religion', but the first 'mythology' (a religion rooted in literary and oral legacies of human relationships and encounters with the divine) and the systems that were able to later result (most of which are still functioning as part of 'normal' everyday life in contemporary society). NABU is the archetypal '*High Priest*' (ENSAG) of the first religion (dedicated to MARDUK) and practiced by priests who preserve the craft of ENKI in *Eridu* with science and 'magic' of the gods to power and sustain the prosperous longevity of *Babylon*.

NAMRASIT *see* NANNA

NAMMTAR *see* NAMTAR

NAMMU *see* TIAMAT

NAMTAR ["*Fate Maker*"]—The 'Black Magici-an', vizier of ERESHKIGAL in the *Underworld*, also likened to the *Assyrian (Chaldean)* plague-god NAMTARU (also the *Akkadian* word for pestilence"). From a ritual text given in *Liber 9* (Tablet-Q in *The Complete Anunnaki Bible*), the priest is to make an image of the affected (sick) person in dough [flour], so as to force the 'plague-god' that afflicts the person to come away from the body and go into the image. The ancient tablets list the name of the plague-god as NAMTARU, and in other places as URA and even URAS (in *Egypt*). In the 'Descent'-cycle, ERESHKIGAL summoned NAMMTAR, the Black Magician, saying these words as she spoke to him: 'Go, NAMMTAR, imprison her [INANNA] in Darkness, in my castle! Release against her the Seven Anunnaki Judges! Release against her the Demons of the Deep...' Then, finally, the representation of a 'demon', like the plague-god NAMTARU, was not intended for 'worship' or 'veneration' (as we might see glorified among today's misguided attempts toward 'dark paths') as a deity. Such statuary typically was constructed only to be 'ceremonially' annihilated or buried as a 'ward' against what the statue (deity) represented.

NAMTARU *see* NAMTAR

NANNA {30}—The official lunar deity of the Enlilite *Sumerian* Anunnaki pantheon, the moon-god, reigning with his feminine lunar consort, NINGAL. An Anunnaki designation of 30 is significant to the approximate number of days in a month; whereby the original Sumerian calendar consists of twelve cycles of 30 days for a 360 day year (and the reason a circle is divided into 360 degrees). NANNA and NINGAL begot the twins: INANNA and SAMAS; mythographically, the *moon* gave birth to the *sun* and V*enus* is a twin-star to the *sun*. To the ancient, the moon was the 'sun-at-night'. It illuminated the pathway for travelers and kept 'watch' as the people slept. Just as the sun is invoked to grant judgments of the daytime [see SAMAS], the moon is given domain of the night and *dreamscapes* (including the 'astral plane'). The day, "Monday", is obviously named after the moon, and is likewise sacred. The essence and color of silver is usually corresponded.

NANNAR *see* NANNA

NEBO *see* NABU

NERGAL {8}—The official spouse (consort) of ERESHKIGAL ('*Queen of the Underworld*'). NERGAL corresponds to the symbol and energetic current of *Mars,* with a fiery and destructive nature commemorated in the *Babylonian* epithet ERRA ("*Annihilator*"). The vitality and raw power of *Mars* (ruling Tuesday) is evident in the essences: iron and blood.

NINAGAL—An epithet meaning "*Prince of the Great Waters*," the name appears for a son of ENKI, who in the *Ziusurda* (*Atra-Asis*) cycle is selected by ENKI to navigate the archetypal "ark" sea-craft during the Great Flood.

NINANNA *see* INANNA

NINGAL {25} ["*Great Lady*"]—The daughter of ENKI; espoused (consort) to NANNA (SIN) and the mother of INANNA (ISHTAR) and SAMAS.

NINGISHZIDA—The 'Lord of the Tree of Life', a son of ENKI and brother to MARDUK, known as *Hermes* and *Thoth-the-Elder* (or TUTU) in a time before NABU. He is a geneticist, trained under ENKI in the arts of life engineering (and reality engineering) that was later taught by NABU (*Thoth-the-Younger* or TUTU) and it evolved into the mystical school of 'Hermetics' (or 'Hermeticism'). Having lost in the 'Pyramid Wars' (c. 3400 B.C. to 3150 B.C.) against MARDUK (RA) and not participating in the pro-MARDUK revolution of ENKI's lineage, NINGISHZIDA establishes his own realm in South America, known by the indigenous people and tradition as QUETZAL-COATL, the 'feather-ed serpent' (literally 'plumed serpent').

NINHARSAG *see* NINHURSAG

NINHURSAG {5}—The chief Anunnaki physician, the mother of NINURTA by ENLIL; a half-sister to ENLIL and ENKI by ANU. In an attempt to produce a royal heir or his own, ENKI even courts her at one time. She is not espoused to any of the pantheon, but instead serves the role of 'birth-goddess' and 'midwife' to the birth and raising of the Anunnaki children (of the Younger Generation), carrying names like MAMMI ("*Mother*") and NINTI ("*Lady of Life*"). When attempting to relieve the toiling of the IGIGI faction of the Anunnaki, ENKI seeks out NINHURSAG to assist in the 'creation' of the 'human' race. Her response, being: 'If ENKI will provide for me the clay, then I will make the creation'. In this antropogenetic cycle, she mixes the clay with the flesh and blood of 'Awmelu' (presumed to be a slain deity). In other versions, the 'essence' is more clearly semen and/or other genetic material. Cuneiform tablet records indicate that six different attempts are made before the '*Adamu*' (the seventh) is fashioned.

NINIB *see* NINURTA

NINKI {35} ["*Lady of the Earth*"]—The official spouse (consort) of ENKI, also known as DAMKINA ["*Lady Who Came to Earth*"]. NINKI is the daughter of ALALU (the 'heavenly' king prior to ANU) and the the mother of MARDUK.

NINLIL {45} "*Lady of Air-Space*"—The official spouse (consort) of ENLIL, also known with the epithet SUD ("nurse"). The background to the relationship between ENLIL and NINLIL is not commonly found in the typical cuneiform tablet cycles. Naturally, the lore is *not* Mardukite or

Babylonian in origin and does not appear in the tablet catalogue or commentary of (modern) Mardukite Core anthologies. The cycle is sometimes referred to as *"Enlil's Banishment to the Underworld."*

NINMAH *see* NINHURSAG

NINSHUBAR *see* NINSHUBUR

NINSHUBUR [*"Lady of the East"*]—Personal assistant (Mercury), second-in-command to the goddess INANNA (ISHTAR). She does not take a consort and there is an alluded love-relationship between her and INANNA (ISHTAR).

NINSUBAR *see* NINSHUBUR

NINTI *see* NINHURSAG

NINTINUGGA *see* BAU

NINTU *see* ARURU

NINURTA {4/(50)} *"Lord of the South Wind"*— The official heir-son of ENLIL, born of ENLIL and NINMAH, espoused to BAU. NINURTA represents the current of Saturn in the Mardukite paradigm, representative both of "hidden power" and "hidden secrets" (an idiom for the dark power and secrets behind the origins and legacy of *Babylon*). In the Enlilite *Sumerian* worldview, NINURTA (called NINIB in *Babylonian*) is the

Enlil-in-waiting, a position usurped by MARDUK proper for the *Age of Aries*. As Enlilship is typically symbolized by 'dragon-slaying', the same motif present in the elevation of MARDUK in *Babylon* rivaling the dragon-queen TIAMAT can be seen in the older *Sumerian* cycles where the prowess of NINURTA is shown in his ability to fight the mighty dragon KUR. His colors are black and violet and his essence corresponds to the metal lead.

NIRGAL *see* NERGAL

NISABA—The *Sumerian* agricultural goddess of writing and scribes; replaced by the god NABU in the Mardukite *Babylonian* Anunnaki tradition.

NUDIMMUD *see* ENKI

NUNAMIR *see* ENLIL

NUSKU ["*Bringer of Light*"]—ENLIL's vizier.

NUZKU *see* NUSKU

OANNES *see* ENKI

RAMMAN(U) *see* ADAD

SAMAS {20}—The official solar deity of the Enlilite *Sumerian* Anunnaki pantheon, brother to IN-ANNA (SHTAR), born of NANNA and NINGAL. The sun represents the brilliance and radiant energy of life on earth; the light that allows organic life to grow and even the manner of which 'time' [and 'lifespan'] is divided. Expansive powerful energy of the solar current is invoked in magical ceremonies for general success and well-being. The fiery nature of the 'star' is called upon to 'incinerate iniquities' and reveal the nature of darkness and lies, meaning: the revelation of truth. Mistaken (by modern scholars) as monotheistic 'sun worship', solar veneration is really the celebration of life. As an archetypal representative of the 'starry' 'heavens', the sun signifies a presence and watchful eye of the 'All-Seeing-God', invoked in matters of law to bring righteous judgment. Sunday is sacred to SAMAS along with the color yellow, and both the color and essence of gold.

SARPANIT {(5)/(45)}—Seventh generation of ADAPA (by ENKI), the chosen royal spouse (consort) of MARDUK; princess-queen patron goddess (ISHTAR) of *Babylon* and mother to NABU. In alternative versions of the lore, her name ERU (or ERUA) designates her as the 'mother-goddess' of the '*Children of MARDUK*' (later associated with the light-folk or elves of Europe).

SHAMMASH *see* SAMAS

SHERIDA *see* AYA

SIN *see* NANNA

SUD *see* NINLIL

SUEN *see* NANNA

TAMMUZ *see* DUMUZI

TEHOM *see* TIAMAT

TIAMAT ["*Life-Giving Mother*"]—The 'primeval dragon' in *Babylonian* archaic epics, often equated with the *Sumerian* KUR. Later esoteric traditions associate 'her' as *Yaldabaoth* (*Ialda-baoth*) in Gnostic Hermeticism, or *Khornozon* (*Choronzon*) in Enochian Hermeticism. She is equated with the 'waters' or the 'Deep' in post-Sumerian Semitic scripture (Hebrew: *tehom*) – the all-encompassing "Sea" is parted to reveal the first 'division' (fragmentation) of "Life" in the Universe. She is paired anthropomorphically with ABZU (the *Abyss*) as the prehistoric 'ancestors' of the Anunnaki race. Her primary literary presence as TIAMAT (or T(I)AMTU) is in the *Enuma Elis* (*Babylonian*) 'Epic of Creation'. In later times, the name is used for the wife of ADAMU (*Adam*), being the equivalent to the Semitic "Eve" character.

TUTU *see* NABU

UDDU/UTTU *see* SAMAS

ZARPANITUM *see* SARPANIT

SYSTEMOLOGY

The Pathway to Self-Honesty

THE WAY INTO THE

FUTURE

A Handbook for the New Human

A collection of writings by
Joshua Free
as selected by James Thomas

*now available as a
Collector's Edition Hardcover*

Here are the basic answers to what has held
Humanity back from achieving its ultimate
goals and unlocking true power of the Spirit
and the highest state of Knowing and Being.

"The Way Into The Future" illuminates the
Pathway leading to Planet Earth's true
"metahuman" destiny. With *excerpts from
"Tablets of Destiny," "Crystal Clear,"
"Systemology—The Original Thesis"* and
"The Power of Zu." You can help shine clear
light on anyone's pathway!

Carefully selected by Mardukite
Publications Officer, James Thomas,
this critical *collection of eighteen
articles, lecture transcripts and reference
chapters* by Joshua Free is sure to be
not only a treasured part
of your personal library,
but also the perfect gift—
an introduction to Systemology
for all friends, family and loved ones.

(*Basic Grade-III Introductory Pocket Anthology*)

SYSTEMOLOGY
The Pathway to Self-Honesty

GO FURTHER AND BE

CRYSTAL CLEAR

JOSHUA FREE

CRYSTAL CLEAR

CRYSTAL CLEAR

(Handbook for Seekers)

Mardukite Systemology Liber-2B
by Joshua Free

now available as a
Revised Academy Edition Hardcover

Take control of your destiny
and chart the first steps
toward your own spiritual evolution.
Realize new potentials of the
Human Condition with
a Self-guiding handbook for
Self-Processing toward
Self-Actualization
in Self-Honesty using actual
techniques and training
provided for the coveted
"Mardukite Systemology Grade-III
Self-Defragmentation Course Program"
—once only available
directly and privately from
the underground Systemology Society.

Discover the amazing power behind the
applied spiritual technology
used for counseling and advisement in
the tradition of Mardukite Zuism.

PUBLISHED BY THE **JOSHUA FREE** IMPRINT REPRESENTING

The Founding Church of Mardukite Zuism

THE JOSHUA FREE IMPRINT
JFI PUBLICATIONS

MARDUKITE
ZUISM

mardukite.com

www.ingramcontent.com/pod-product-compliance
Lightning Source LLC
Chambersburg PA
CBHW011221120626
46545CB00010B/3095